Everything I Learned About How to Publish a Book

V. V. CAM

Disclaimer: The general information provided in this book may not apply to your specific situation. The information is accurate as of the publication date and it is subject to change. All links to websites, companies and service providers are provided for your convenience only. Please consult individual websites for current information regarding their practice, policies and pricing, etc.

The author is neither an attorney nor an accountant. Please consult with the appropriate personnel or agencies in your country for advice on legal and taxation matters.

CONTENTS

1. OUR PUBLISHING JOURNEY 1

2. TO SELF-PUBLISH OR NOT 6

    2.1 What I learned about traditional publishing and self-publishing 12

    2.2 Self-assessment: Is self-publishing right for me? 16

3. BASIC 7 STEPS TO PUBLISH YOUR BOOK 18

    STEP 1 – WRITE YOUR MANUSCRIPT **19**

    3.1 Self-assessment: I want to publish because… 21

    3.2 What I learned about the writing process 22

    3.3 Questions to ask yourself for finding writing inspirations 24

    3.4 Five tips to get started writing 26

    3.5 Links to writing communities 27

    STEP 2 – FIND BETA READERS **29**

    3.6 What I learned about beta readers 30

    3.7 Sample email to a beta reader 32

    3.8 Sample questions for beta readers 33

    3.9 Links to find beta readers 35

    STEP 3 – EDIT YOUR MANUSCRIPT **36**

    3.10 What I learned about the editing process 39

    3.11 Checklist for self-editing process 42

    3.12 Checklist for finding an editor 44

    3.13 Links to editing software 45

    STEP 4 – PROOFREAD YOUR MANUSCRIPT **47**

    3.14 What I learned about the proofreading process 48

    STEP 5 – FORMAT YOUR BOOK **51**

eBook **51**

3.15 What I learned about eBooks 53

3.16 What I learned about formatting an eBook 54

3.17 Checklist for formatting an eBook 55

3.18 What I learned about writing/conversion software......57

3.19 Links to eBook formatting guides 58

Print book **58**

3.20 What I learned about print books..................................59

3.21 Self-assessment: Should I do print books?...................60

3.22 What I learned about formatting a print book 61

3.23 Five steps to format a print book 63

3.24 Checklist for formatting a print book 64

Front and Back Matter...............................**66**

3.25 Front Matter..66

3.26 Back Matter 67

STEP 6 – DESIGN YOUR BOOK COVER **68**

3.27 What I learned about cover design 69

3.28 What I learned about images 71

3.29 Links for images 72

3.30 What I learned about fonts 74

3.31 Links for fonts 75

3.32 Checklist for cover design..75

3.33 Links for cover designers 77

STEP 7 – PUBLISH YOUR BOOK **78**

Distribution..**78**

3.34 Amazon's KDP (Kindle Direct Publishing) Select 79

3.35 What I learned about KDP Select 81

3.36 eBook retailers 83

3.37 POD book distributors..84

3.38 Aggregators........ 85

3.39 Printing services...89

3.40 What I learned about printing services 89

3.41 Links to printing services 90

3.42 What I learned about distribution..91

BOOK DESCRIPTION/BLURB **93**

3.43 What I learned about book description/blurb 95

KEYWORDS AND CATEGORIES **99**

3.44 What I learned about keywords 100

3.45 What I learned about categories...101

3.46 Links to sites for keywords research tools 102

PRICING **102**

3.47 What I learned about pricing..103

INTERNATIONAL STANDARD BOOK NUMBER (ISBN)........**108**

3.48 What I learned about ISBN 108

3.49 Links to sites for ISBNs...111

COPYRIGHT...**111**

3.50 What I learned about copyright 111

DIGITAL RIGHTS MANAGEMENT (DRM) **112**

3.51 What I learned about DRM..113

4. WEBSITES 114

AUTHOR WEBSITE...**114**

4.1   What I learned about creating an author website.......................117

4.2　Five steps to creating your author website 119

4.3　Links for web hosting services 120

4.4　Links for free website-building platforms 120

4.5　Links for website-building tutorials 121

4.6　Checklist for building an author website 121

AMAZON AUTHOR CENTRAL **122**

4.7　What I learned about Amazon Author Central 123

GOODREADS **125**

4.8　What I learned about Goodreads 125

5.　PUBLISHING CHECKLISTS 127

5.1　PRE-PUBLISHING **127**

5.2　PUBLISHING **128**

5.3　POST-PUBLISHING **130**

6.　SALES & EARNINGS REPORTS 132

6.1　What I learned about sales and earnings 133

7.　EQUIPMENT & TOOLS 135

8.　PUBLISHING COSTS 139

9.　MISCELLANEOUS 142

WORKING WITH OTHERS **142**

CATALOGUING IN PUBLICATION (CIP) **144**

CANADIAN AUTHORS **144**

9.1　What I learned about CIP 145

9.2　List of steps to get your CIP 145

US AUTHORS **146**

LEGAL DEPOSIT REQUIREMENT FOR CANADIAN PUBLISHERS..**146**

9.3   Links for Legal Deposit...148

USEFUL LINKS **148**

FILE STORAGE AND SHARING 148

FREELANCE MARKETPLACES...149

IDEA GENERATORS 150

LINK SHORTENERS, BACKLINKS AND UNIVERSAL LINKS 150

MONITORING TOOLS 150

PLAGIARISM CHECKERS 151

PRODUCTIVITY TOOLS...152

REFERENCE TOOLS 152

RESEARCH TOOLS 153

TRACKING AND TESTING RESOURCES 154

VALIDATOR 154

WORD COUNTER...155

ALL THE BEST WITH YOUR PUBLISHING JOURNEY 156

ACKNOWLEDGEMENTS...158

ABOUT THE AUTHOR...159

INDEX 161

1. OUR PUBLISHING JOURNEY

A few years ago, I knew absolutely nothing about the publishing world. After spending countless hours researching and learning, I was able to help my husband publish and promote his book on bestseller lists in multiple categories on Amazon, get it into over a hundred libraries, and have it translated into Chinese.

If you are reading this book, I assume you are either thinking of having your work published or are interested in knowing more about publishing. I want to help you pursue your own writing dream with the knowledge and confidence you need to succeed. My husband and I have learned a lot about self-publishing during these past few years, and we wish to share our experience with others embarking on their own self-publishing journey.

In this book, I will point out those little things that you'll want to know and give you all the tools, checklists, and templates that I have collected or created during our publishing journey. I hope these tools will make your own self-publishing experience better. My intention is to save you time, money, and confusion by outlining everything you need to know as succinctly as possible.

If you've read other books on self-publishing, you will notice that this book includes similar information. However, you may notice the following differences:

- Although at times it may be necessary to describe the steps needed to complete a certain task, this book focuses more on the publishing process itself. Tutorials and how-to information are readily available and you will get more up-to-date instructions through the Internet than from a book.

- The world is full of information and advice, but I've made sure to include only the most practical and relevant content. I present it to you in an unbiased manner so you can reach your own conclusions and decisions.

- The book is organized so that you can read it straight through and follow the steps in order. Alternatively, you can use it as a reference manual and find all the related information in individual sections as you need it.

The information in this book is current at the time of publication. The self-publishing industry will continue to evolve and improve, so certain tools, practices, and resources may change or cease to exist at any given time. For that very reason, I did not include information on how to navigate websites or how to use the tools. Instead, I included the principles and my personal experiences to guide you through the process.

I'll always remember how our journey began and the excitement and nervousness we felt when we released something we'd created into the world. We are still amazed at the profound effect publishing a book has had on us. When we hold our book in our hands, we feel a sense of pride, a sense of achievement. Together we created something miraculous that meant so much to the both of us, almost like having a child who never ceases to bring us smiles and happiness.

I've got to tell you that I find it incredibly exciting that in this day and age, anyone can self-publish. Self-publishing can be amazing if you know how to do it properly, but the process is not always intuitive or easy. I have gone through the process, come up with a set of practices that worked best for me, and I want to share my knowledge and experiences with you.

There are two books in the *Because Self-Publishing Works* series (http://www.because.zone/because-self-publishing-works):

Book 1: Everything I Learned About How to Publish a Book

Book 2: Everything I Learned About How to Market a Book

Each book stands alone. Book 1 covers the process of self-publishing while Book 2 covers the marketing aspects of self-publishing. If you are only interested in getting your book published, Book 1 is all you will need. If you want to grow your self-publishing business, then Book 2 will be more suitable.

In this book, I focus mainly on direct self-publishing of fictional work through Amazon, simply because it is the platform that my husband and I concentrate our publishing efforts on. However, you can use the same process with other platforms.

Let's get started on your publishing journey!

2. TO SELF-PUBLISH OR NOT

Before a word was written, my husband, Jack, asked if we were going to publish like his friend, who got her book published through a publisher after many years and numerous rejections. We had been wanting to do a project together—something to leave our mark on this world. Writing a book seemed the perfect way to do that. However, it dawned on me that I didn't have a clue about publishing. I definitely needed do some research.

After many hours of consulting with the Internet, I found so much information on the subject! Equipped with my newfound knowledge, I was excited to tell Jack what I'd discovered. This is when I learned about self-publishing: a process which allows the author to control the entire creative and selling process. I found the fact that people could now write books and publish them themselves absolutely fascinating.

In fact, self-publishing has been around for a long time, but has only become more common since the late 90s. Before this time, most books were published in the traditional way, by submitting a manuscript to an agent who in turn submits it to a publisher. After a contract is signed, the book will then go through more edits and eventually be published. In contrast, self-publishing combines author, agent, and publisher roles into one—an independent or indie author.

"Sounds like self-publishing means we have to do everything ourselves," Jack said.

"Well, no. The 'self' refers to being able to rely on your own self. You can choose to do everything if you wish, but you can also hire others to help you."

"It still sounds like it would require a lot of work. I don't think I'd feel fully 'validated' being a self-published author."

"What doesn't require a lot of work?" I laughed. I mentioned something about times changing fast and isn't it nice that we now have so many tools and platforms to choose from?

I could tell that he needed more convincing, so I continued, "Yes, it is true that if one of the recognizable publishers picks and publishes our work, it will make us feel that our work is good enough. But getting there is a long process that involves many submissions and rejections from agents and publishers. It could take years before our book gets published. Or…we could make our book available for sale within four to 72 hours."

Then Jack said, "But if we publish the traditional way, the financial reward is good. Plus, we don't have to come up with any money up front."

"It's true that we don't have to pay anyone in a traditional publishing deal, but it requires upfront time investment. Also, the average author usually receives an advance and an average of 10% royalties of net book price. The royalties earned above the advance amount will be paid six months later. On the other hand, self-publishing may require a small upfront financial investment, but when we self-publish, we will earn up to 70% profit on sales and get paid in just 60 days.

"Besides, there are other advantages when we self-publish. As indie authors, we have total creative control over our content and design. In traditional publishing we would hand over control to the publisher, who might impose editorial choices. After signing a contract, traditionally published authors have almost zero control over pricing, timing of publication, or marketing. Sometimes the cover, the title, and even the words themselves are out of their hands. When we self-publish, we can work with freelancers of our choice, and we can choose the ultimate look and feel of our book. We have the ability to decide the marketing strategy from beginning to end— what is written, when it's published, the cover, blurb, price, advertising, etc. If something needs changing, we can change it without having to ask anyone for permission."

"So what are the disadvantages if we self-publish, then?" Jack asked.

"Well, did I say that there will be lots of work? As we are new to the business, it's a steep learning curve to learn the whole process, including writing, publishing and marketing—being both the author and publisher. We may have to find and work with people to produce our book. This will be a problem if we don't have the time or don't enjoy doing everything."

Then I added with a smile, "Good thing I love being an entrepreneur. I have the technical skills and I love to learn the marketing and publishing sides of things. I can help publish and market our book. All you have to do is write."

"Marketing? Isn't this typically a publisher's job if the book is traditionally published?"

"Marketing effort provided by publishers is usually related to how much is invested in the project, and it is usually to booksellers rather than consumers. Nowadays, traditional authors have to do their own marketing, as agents and publishers will often seek out those who have an established presence and existing readership. As indie authors, we will be 100 percent responsible for promoting our work."

At this point, he asked me if we needed to consider anything else if we were going to self-publish.

"Unless we just want to publish and don't care whether we make a sale or not, we need to be willing to do what it takes to create a professional product if we want to be successful. To make publishing into a business, we will need to invest in it and treat and run it as such. We can make money if we get everything right and keep working away—writing, publishing, and marketing—repeatedly.

"Then we also need to be interested in running a small business. There is more to self-publishing than uploading a file to a retailer's site and gaining profits. We will be responsible for all of the things a publisher does, such as content editing, line editing, proofreading, formatting, cover design, distribution, marketing, legal, accounting, and taxes. We will need to have the necessary skills, equipment, and tools to conduct business online.

"We also need to be realistic about the risk we are willing to take. We will have to come up with money for editing and proofreading, cover art, and all the expenses that come with self-publishing if we are going to hire others. When we self-publish, there is no one else to absorb the risk of publication."

At this point, my husband asked me if we had to choose which way to go.

"No," was my answer. "The industry is changing quickly, and many authors now take a hybrid approach to publishing. Did you know that there are publishers canvassing self-published authors, and some of the best-selling books started out as self-published books?

So I think since neither option comes with a single guarantee of success, why don't we use self-publishing to get into the business? And if we do well, agents and publishers will come to us. But first you need to write the book, my dear."

2.1   What I learned about traditional publishing and self-publishing

- You can try to get your book traditionally published, but your work may never be accepted by an agent and/or a publisher. After finishing your book, it might take a year or two to get an agent, then another year to get a publishing deal from a publisher. It could be another six months to two and a half years before your book is finally launched. You can publish the book yourself and have it available for sale within four to 72 hours.

- You will need to deal with potentially restrictive or problematic contract clauses in traditional publishing deals. It is likely that you will need to hire a lawyer to look over the contract to make sure the terms and conditions, including royalties and rights, are suitable for you. A book is an intellectual property asset that can earn money for the life of the author and 70 years after his death. In self-publishing, there is no contract with a publisher, and you retain all your rights.

- You don't need to pay upfront if you are going to publish traditionally. Publishing companies will assign an editor, a cover designer, and a formatter to work on your book. When you self-publish, you will need to hire and pay for your own editor, cover designer, and formatter if you don't have these skills. If you do these tasks yourself, it may be less expensive and faster when changes are needed, but the result may not be up to acceptable standards. You will also need to have the necessary skills, equipment, and tools to conduct business online.

- You can shoestring it and do everything yourself and not spend a dime on producing your book, or you can outsource part of or the entire publishing process.

- Traditionally published authors have almost zero control over pricing, timing of publication, marketing, sometimes over the cover, the title, and even the words themselves. When you self-publish, you have total creative control over your content and design, and you can make changes to everything at any time without having to ask anyone for permission. But you also have to deal with issues such as making sure you haven't violated anyone else's copyright or infringed on any trademarks, as well as getting appropriate permissions when needed.

- The average author usually receives an advance of less than $10,000 and between 7% and 25% (averaging 10%) of net book price in royalties. Discounts, returns, marketing costs, and overhead are taken off the total before your percentage is calculated. For example, if you get an advance of $10,000, you have to earn more than $10,000 in book royalties before you make any more money. Royalties are usually paid every six months. On the other hand, if you self-publish and set your book price between $2.99 and $9.99 on Amazon, you get a 70% profit (35% for other prices and markets) on book sales in 60 days. There are self-published authors making under $100 per year and some making five- and six-figure incomes every month.

- Traditionally published books are included in catalogues and distribution channels recognized by bookstores and libraries. Publishers also have sales representatives who market books to brick-and-mortar stores and make it very easy for book buyers to select books. Books are usually in the stores for a month and only remain there if they sell consistently. While it is harder to get self-published books displayed in stores, it is easy to make them available for stores and libraries to purchase through distributors.

- Literary prizes and critical acclaim are more likely through traditional publishing.

- You will need to promote your work whether you go the traditional route or the self- publishing one. So regardless of how you publish, you will need to learn about marketing if you want sales.

- You may choose to use self-publishing to get into the business, and if you do well, agents and publishers may come to sign a publishing deal with you.

- The beauty of self-publishing is that it's your decision to make. You make the call, take the risks, and reap the rewards. It is an industry with a very low cost of entry, allowing you the opportunity to do it on your own terms.

- Of course, you will need to write something first before you can publish either way.

2.2   Self-assessment: Is self-publishing right for me?

☐ Am I willing to learn? It's a steep learning curve to learn the whole process, including writing, marketing, and publishing.

☐ Do I have the time? Will I enjoy doing this? I may have to find and work with people to produce the book. I will need the time to do everything.

☐ Will I be willing to invest? I need a budget upfront if I want professional result. It is possible to produce a book with zero financial investment, but if I am intending to make a living from this, then I will need to invest money.

☐ Am I capable and willing to do what it takes? I will be responsible for all of the things a publisher does: editing, proofreading, formatting, cover design, distribution, marketing, legal issues, accounting, taxes, etc.

☐ Am I comfortable with communicating and working with others? I may need to contact and work with other people to get things done, to get my book into stores or to present my book to groups, etc.

☐ Do I have the necessary equipment and tools I need?

☐ Am I willing to take the risk? When I self-publish, there is no one else but me to absorb the risk of publication. Everything that has to be done to publish a book is something I have to pay for in one way or another.

☐ Do I know my goal and my definition of success? What does success look like to me? I will consider what's important to me and determine how I am going to measure that success so that I know when and whether I achieve my goal.

☐ If my goal is to make money, do I have a business plan? What is my financial goal in realistic and measurable terms?

Downloadable Item

2.2-Self-assessment: Is self-publishing right for me?
Log in: https://goo.gl/gb2ata or **Sign up:** https://goo.gl/XxrEro

3. BASIC 7 STEPS TO PUBLISH YOUR BOOK

Here are the basic seven steps to get your book published. You will find useful details, tips, and various samples and resources for each of the step in the following chapters.

1. Write your manuscript

2. Find beta readers to read and give feedback on your manuscript

3. Edit your manuscript

4. Proofread your manuscript

5. Format your book

6. Design a cover for your book

7. Publish your book on different online retailers

STEP 1 – WRITE YOUR MANUSCRIPT

It took Jack a couple of years to write his 150,000-word (379-page, 6" by 9" print book) debut novel, *because* (http://www.because.zone). It's an inspirational novel about one man's journey to find his purpose and learn to live again after a tragic accident.

Although Jack's book is fictional, much of the story is based on his incredible adventures working in schools and with people that live with a passion to help others. As a first-time writer, it was easier for him to write about something he was familiar with and passionate about.

While he was writing his book, every night when I came home from work Jack would read what he'd written during the day to me. I always remember how we enjoyed our conversations we had that led to more ideas and more conversations. There was always something for us to talk about.

But there were challenges, too. Jack would often get what is commonly known as 'writer's block,' rendering him unable to proceed with his writing for days at a time. When he tried to write, his sentences would run too long, his dialogue would sound too stilted, and his writing would feel disjointed. He would find himself unsatisfied with his writing and delete an entire day's work in frustration.

When I held our book in my hands for the first time, the first thought that crossed my mind was: *We did it!* Jack had captured his own real-life experiences through a world of his own creation. Writing a book wasn't easy—it took a great deal of dedication, perseverance, and commitment. Nevertheless, we believe the end result was worth every ounce of blood, sweat, and fears.

If you are reading this book, you probably have a unique story, talent, or idea that you want to share. And I believe that if you want to use your words to change the world in a positive way, there is no better time than now to write and publish your book. Take a few minutes to do the self-assessment below. If you decide there is no reason for you to publish, spend your time where you feel joyful, creative, and alive.

And if you can find one or two reasons to venture into the publishing world—whether you want to write for your mind, your heart, your wallet, or for the betterment of humankind—enjoy the journey you are about to begin, because it can be incredibly exciting and rewarding!

3.1 Self-assessment: I want to publish because…

- ☐ I want to tell others about my experiences.
- ☐ I want to feel good about myself.
- ☐ I want to leave a legacy.
- ☐ I want to give others insight into what I do or who I am.
- ☐ I want to achieve something tangible.
- ☐ I want to help others overcome their challenges.
- ☐ I want to share my good fortune or knowledge with others.
- ☐ I want to bring comfort to others.
- ☐ I want to encourage others to do something.
- ☐ I want to impact others in some way.
- ☐ I want to make others aware of something.
- ☐ I want to bring hope and happiness to others.
- ☐ I want to make others laugh.
- ☐ I want to solidify my brand.
- ☐ I want to give my writing as a gift.
- ☐ I have the solution to others' problems.

- ☐ I want to demonstrate my knowledge or expertise.

- ☐ I want to increase my business credibility.

- ☐ I want to distinguish myself from my competitors.

- ☐ I want to become an expert in my field.

- ☐ I want to be a leader in my industry.

- ☐ I want to generate passive income from writing.

- ☐ I want to introduce new concepts to others.

- ☐ I want to start a new career as an author.

- ☐ I want to promote a worthy cause.

- ☐ I want to fulfill a life goal.

- ☐ I want to…

Downloadable Item

3.1-Self-assessment: I want to publish because…

Log in: https://goo.gl/gb2ata or **Sign up:** https://goo.gl/XxrEro

3.2   What I learned about the writing process

- You can start your publishing journey with a short manuscript. Although there are no firm rules about length, fictional short stories are often under 8,000 words (approximately 20 pages). If your manuscript falls between 8,000 and 20,000 words, it's a novelette. If your manuscript falls between 20,000 and 40,000 words, it's a novella. A manuscript over 40,000 words is considered a novel.

- You can write the book yourself or hire a ghostwriter to write it for you. A professional ghostwriter can bring your story to life, but it will still be yours. You will be credited as the author, you will keep all the rights, and you will receive all profits from sales.

- You will need to do some research, and the amount of research depends on how much you already know about your subject. Facts are important, especially in nonfiction works where incorrect information could be detrimental to your readers and your credibility. Unless your work of fiction is based in a fantasy world, you will need to do a lot of research to get all the facts right and to build a believable story. Staying consistent and true to what you have created is crucial.

- You will need to learn how to craft a story in a coherent manner that involves a lot more than story structure, character development, plotting, and point of view. Pick a topic or idea that you can write about with energy and interest.

- You will get better and more efficient if you write consistently. Set specific, feasible, and time-oriented goals and make sure to follow through. For example, *I will write 1,000 words a day* or *I will write 30 minutes each day.*

- There are numerous writing communities and critique groups that you can join for ideas, inspirations, and critique, both offline and online.

3.3   Questions to ask yourself for finding writing inspirations

- What are the things that I enjoy doing or am passionate about that I can turn into a book that entertains, educates, and/or inspires other people?

- When I am in a bookstore, what genres or titles seem to draw me in? Could I write a similar book?

- When I read reviews of the books and movies that I am interested in, what topics or gaps do they reveal that I could write about?

- What topics are people currently discussing on TV or the radio? Do I have any opinions or thoughts on these matters, and could I create a story revolving around these subjects?

- What songs or movies inspire me to write about something?

- What's trending? Check out http://google.com/trends for fresh ideas.

- What is something that I am interested in but have not been able to find in a book?

- What is something that I could research and write about? (http://howstuffworks.com)

- What do people often come to me for help or advice about?

- What are the types of fairs or events that interest me? Could I write about them?

- What outdated books or books in public domain could I update or adapt with my own view and style? (http://gutenberg.org)

- What are the common questions people ask or things they search for on the Internet that I could research and write about? (http://answers.yahoo.com)

- What writer's group could I join to get ideas or discuss topics that I could write about?

- How can I turn what people post on social media into compelling stories? (http://storify.com)

3.4 Five tips to get started writing

1. Pick a topic that you are interested in or passionate about, start writing your first sentence, and then stretch it out to a paragraph. Write an outline for fiction and write a table of contents with different sections for nonfiction in order of beginning, middle, and end. Start to fill the gaps in between.

2. Set a realistic, attainable daily word count goal and spend dedicated time writing in a designated place every day. For now, just write anything, as long as you are writing something. Slowly increase your word count once you start building momentum. Keep track of your daily accomplishments. Celebrate the progress you've made while still being honest with yourself about how much work is left to do. Whenever you stop writing for the day, stop mid-sentence, as it is easier to finish a half-written

sentence than to start a new one from scratch the next day.

3. Write down or use a recorder to capture your ideas and inspirations whenever and wherever you can.

4. Find someone who will give you honest feedback on your writing early on to help you see if you are headed in the right direction.

5. Commit to a deadline and publishing schedule. Your first book may not be perfect, but there are many opportunities to learn and try again.

3.5   Links to writing communities

- Absolute Write

  http://absolutewrite.com

- Booksie

  https://www.booksie.com

- Critique Circle

  http://www.critiquecircle.com

- Critters Workshop

  http://www.critters.org

- KBoards

  http://www.kboards.com/index.php/board,60.0.html

- NaNoWriMo

  http://nanowrimo.org

- Protagonize

  http://www.protagonize.com/

- Scribophile

  http://www.scribophile.com

- Scriggler

  https://scriggler.com

- Wattpad

  https://www.wattpad.com

- WritersCafe

  http://www.writerscafe.org

- Writing.com

  https://www.writing.com

STEP 2 – FIND BETA READERS

When Jack finished the final draft of his novel, we found seven beta readers to help spot flaws and point out problems with continuity and plausibility.

I sent emails to a few people after I got their contact information on a forum, and two agreed to beta read for us. I found the remaining beta readers through a company that provides a beta reading service.

Our beta readers were wonderful, avid readers. They read the entire manuscript and provided honest personal reactions and suggestions to improve the story, characters, and settings. Some found grammar issues, spelling, and typos. One even helped with fact-checking.

The most challenging part for us was to go against some of the suggestions. It was difficult because although the suggestions were candid, some were based on personal preferences and would have required the book to be rewritten a certain way.

3.6   What I learned about beta readers

- Beta readers usually are avid readers who are not trained as editors. They can even be friends or family. Some beta readers will help you out for free while others will charge a small fee. Reading and commenting on a whole book is a big commitment, so some free beta readers will never finish. Getting beta readers to read your draft is a great first step and will save you some money at editing time.

- Find a minimum of two to four beta readers, with at least one who would be interested in your type of book. Ideally, find one beta reader who knows more about writing craft than you do. You will want to find beta readers that aren't afraid to express their honest opinions in a kind way.

- You can find free beta readers through your social media networks, writing communities, and forums, or you can hire them from one of the many beta reader services available.

- Provide your beta readers the best version of your manuscript that you have in the format they prefer.

- Let your beta readers know when and what kind of feedback you would like to receive from them. You can create and send a list of questions you want answers to, or you can create Google Forms and insert hyperlinks within key points of your book for their feedback.

- You will receive different and sometimes conflicting suggestions. Some of the feedback will provide insight and inspiration you can use to improve your story. Other feedback may be less helpful. In that case, simply acknowledge their ideas and thank them. But, if you receive the same feedback from multiple beta readers, carefully review that issue before dismissing it.

- Always be grateful to your beta readers. If it is feasible, mention their names in your acknowledgement section.

3.7   Sample email to a beta reader

Subject: Beta Reader Request

Hello [name if known],

I got your name from [website] and I was wondering if you would be interested in helping to beta read my husband's book. It's a fictional novel of approximately 150K words and here's a brief description:

Throughout his personal and professional life, Robert Sanchez has reached some of the highest mountains on earth and had helped and guided many people to live more fulfilling lives. No one was prepared for the tragic accident that left him physically and emotionally damaged. Although he escaped death, Robert was trapped in his own past, unable to return to his new and different life. It would take a lot more than wisdom, patience and courage to set him free.

Would you please let me know? Thank you in advance for your consideration.

Thank you so much for your time!

V.

3.8   Sample questions for beta readers

- ☐ Does the opening (i.e. first line, paragraph, page and/or chapter) draw you into the story?

- ☐ Did you connect with the characters and care what happens to them? Did you love (or love to hate) the appropriate characters? If not, can you explain why?

- ☐ Could you relate to the main character? Did you feel her/his pain or excitement?

- ☐ Was the dialogue believable, appropriate for the story, natural or overly narrative? Did it remain consistent throughout the story?

- ☐ Did you have trouble visualizing the scenery, clothing, architecture, etc.?

- ☐ Are the plot twists believable, yet unexpected?

- ☐ Was there any place in the book that you lost focus while reading? If so, when and why?

- ☐ Did you notice any discrepancies or inconsistencies in time sequences, places, character details, or other details?

- ☐ Does the story move along without rushing or dragging?

☐ Was there enough conflict, tension, and intrigue to keep your interest?

☐ Were there too many characters to keep track of? Did you get confused about who's who?

☐ Did you feel there was too much or not enough description or explanation?

☐ Did any parts of the book feel unnecessary?

☐ Were you emotionally satisfied at the end?

☐ Do you think the writing style suits the genre? If not, why not?

☐ Would you recommend this book? Are there any issues that would prevent you from purchasing or recommending this book?

☐ Did you have trouble focusing on the storyline due to any editing issues (i.e. punctuation, capitalization, and spelling)?

Downloadable Item

3.8-Beta Reader Questionnaire
Log in: https://goo.gl/gb2ata or **Sign up:** https://goo.gl/XxrEro

3.9   Links to find beta readers

- KBoards

  https://www.kboards.com/yp/index.php/?p_search=bet

  a&action=search

- Goodreads

  https://www.goodreads.com/group/show/50920-beta-

  reader-group

- Quiethouse Editing

  http://www.quiethouseediting.com

- Scribofile

  http://www.scribophile.com

STEP 3 – EDIT YOUR MANUSCRIPT

Before Jack sent his manuscript out into the world, he worked with a couple of editors who shed new light on his work that enabled him to see it from different angles. Their comments helped him to capitalize on his manuscript's strengths and root out certain problems.

At first we had difficulty finding an editor. After finding four different editors through the Internet and sending each the first few chapters, I received their sample edits. Each editor suggested different edits—some of which were conflicting or did not convey Jack's intentions at all. Worse yet, one person's suggestions would have destroyed Jack's writing voice. I was disappointed and confused.

Finally, I found two editors to work on Jack's book. Though using two editors cost more, they helped make the book the best it could be.

You will need to know what kind of editing you're looking for. There are three types of editing:

- Developmental editing is "big-picture" feedback about structure, style, pacing, and voice. Often, a developmental edit is given in the form of a detailed report or letter rather than as notes made directly on the manuscript.

- Line editing is when your editor will point out specific things such as lines of dialogue that don't sound convincing, or pacing problems in a scene. Often, the same editor provides both developmental feedback and line edits. Because developmental feedback assumes the writer will rewrite parts of the manuscript, line editing is sometimes saved until after the rewrite. Alternatively, you might contract an editor to work on a second line edit of the book to address anything added or changed during revisions.

- Copy editing is about fixing errors in grammar, punctuation, spelling, word choice, and sentence structure, as well as catching continuity issues. If you just want the writing "cleaned up," and not any content or structure changes, then you are looking for copy editing.

Here's an example of the developmental editing feedback from one of our editors for Jack's book:

"Present Day – Robert and Monique Sanchez" | Pages 5-6

Synopsis

In this sad chapter, we meet Robert's wife Monique, who is driving him somewhere and trying to connect with him as she drives. The song that used to help her connect with him, "Landslide," doesn't seem to be working for her this time and the reader is left with the sense of a deep distance between husband and wife. Based on comments made in the chapter, we learn that somehow this story has to do with mountain climbing and the comment that the song "Landslide" might somehow now be offensive to Robert makes the reader wonder if there was a climbing accident of some sort. Lingering questions:

- What is Monique and Robert's marriage like? They seem distanced, but why?

- Where are they driving to?

Impressions

(1) The introduction to Monique in this chapter was great. In a very short period of time, I had a nice impression of her personality: optimistic, long-suffering, unselfish, patient

(2) I don't have a solid picture of Monique from this introduction. What does she look like?

(3) I liked the humour of this chapter. I laughed out loud as I read it because I think most people who've ever heard "Landslide" are left wondering what it's about. Using a song that many can relate to was a nice way to create commonality with the reader from the beginning.

3.10   What I learned about the editing process

- It is impossible to edit your own work. You will tend to overlook mistakes because your mind subconsciously fills in what it thinks should be there. Going through the self-editing process multiple times is necessary, but it can actually tempt you to change things that don't need to be changed.

- You can find an assessment business to assess or evaluate your manuscript so that you can correct major problems before you hire an editor. You will receive a report of one or more pages depending on the length of your manuscript and how much work it needs.

- There are many ways to find reliable editors. You can contact your local, state/province, or national editors' associations. You can also solicit recommendations from other writers, librarians, or indie bookstore owners. You should also do an Internet search for editors' websites that appeal to you.

- Hire an editor when you have made the book the best you possibly can on your own. Make sure you've addressed all developmental and line edits before copy edits.

- Tell your editor what you want your book to accomplish so he/she can help you get there.

- Don't expect an editor to do extensive research for you or to invent characters, flesh out dialogue, or write missing scenes.

- Your editor is likely to feel more invested in the kind of book he/she enjoys reading.

- Find an editor who exhibits genuine excitement about your project and your type of book.

- Prepare yourself for feedback, criticism, and direction. When you receive the kind of feedback that you didn't expect, it can be hard to hear, but rather than just dismissing it, you can brainstorm solutions with your editor.

- You can absolutely question or overrule your editor's edits or ask others for their opinions.

- Find an editor who will explain his/her rationale for the edits so that you can learn from the process and truly make the most of your investment.

- Expect the editing process to take time. It is reasonable to allow one week for every 40,000 words. Schedule at least four weeks for editing time and rewrites.

- Editing cost varies between editors, depending upon the kinds of editing you require, the editor's rate (which may be either an hourly rate or a flat fee, usually charged per page), and the number of revisions and rounds of editing. An editor will often ask for a 50% deposit up front before he/she begins with the balance due on completion.

- If you have marketable skills, you could ask your editor if he/she would consider trading your skills for editing.

- You have the option of crediting your editor.

3.11   Checklist for self-editing process

Before sending your manuscript to your editor, you should go through the self-editing process a few times. It's a good practice to save different versions when you make major changes to your manuscript. Always keep backups so you can return to an older version if you change your mind.

Questions to ask during the editing process:

- ☐ After reading the entire manuscript, what is the overall sense of how I constructed and organized the manuscript?

- ☐ Are there any gaps (e.g. jumping from one topic to another without appropriate segue or explanation)?
- ☐ Is my voice consistent throughout?
- ☐ Does every section/chapter deliver on its promise?
- ☐ Is there anything that interferes with the reading experience (e.g. too many examples, quotes, stories, background or technical information, etc.)?
- ☐ Are there too many repetitions of words or phrases?
- ☐ Are my sentences and paragraphs varied in lengths?
- ☐ Is there too much passive voice?
- ☐ Are there too many long paragraphs?
- ☐ Are there too many adjectives or adverbs?
- ☐ Are numbers, capitalization, comma usage, verb tenses, etc. consistent?
- ☐ Are there spelling, punctuation, and grammatical errors?
- ☐ Does it speak to my ideal reader?
- ☐ Does it deliver the objectives I want for my ideal reader?
- ☐ Does it achieve my business and personal objectives?

3.12   Checklist for finding an editor

- ☐ Did the editor respond to my inquiry within a week? If not, chances are that he/she is either swamped and doesn't have time to take on a new client or that he/she isn't very reliable or dedicated.

- ☐ Does the editor provide the editing level I need?

- ☐ Do I feel comfortable with him/her?

- ☐ Did he/she display a good grasp of grammar in his/her responses, website, etc.?

- ☐ Can he/she give me a list of other authors for references?

- ☐ What types of books has he/she edited?

- ☐ What credentials does he/she have?

- ☐ Does the editor confirm which version of English (Canadian, UK/Australian or US) is to be used?

- ☐ Does the editor confirm how many passes he/she would go through the manuscript?

- ☐ Do I understand the final cost and payment terms?

☐ Will he/she provide a free sample edit? This lets me see a real-life example of how he/she edits and gives a good indication as to whether or not we will work well together.

☐ Will he/she be okay with my writing style even though he/she may not agree (for example, ellipses, emphasis, abbreviation, etc.)?

☐ Am I okay with the frequency and method that he/she will be communicating with me?

☐ Am I okay with the length of time he/she will be working on my project?

Downloadable Item

3.12-Checklist for finding an editor

Log in: https://goo.gl/gb2ata or **Sign up:** https://goo.gl/XxrEro

3.13   Links to editing software

These are software programs you can use to help self-edit your manuscript before sending it off to your editor.

- AutoCrit

  https://www.autocrit.com

- Grammarly

  https://www.grammarly.com

- Slick Write

  https://www.slickwrite.com

STEP 4 – PROOFREAD YOUR MANUSCRIPT

Proofreading is an important step. It helps to find and correct typographical errors and mistakes in grammar, style, and spelling. I've asked a couple of friends to go through Jack's book various times to make sure we catch all the errors. When the book was first printed, we ordered a few copies and were so excited to give our real-estate-agent-turned-friend a copy to read. She came back a few days later and told us that she loved the story and said perhaps we should get it edited because there were many mistakes! I couldn't believe what I'd heard and asked her to make note of them for me. I was shocked when I saw all the sticky notes sticking out on almost every page, marking missing words, double words, typos, misplaced punctuation marks—all of which had been missed by a dozen of us including our beta readers and editors. Luckily, I was able to fix all the errors and upload the files again on the same day.

3.14   What I learned about the proofreading process

- Proofread after the editing process. Don't make corrections at the sentence and word level if you still need to work on the focus, organization, and development of the whole manuscript, individual sections, or even paragraphs.

- Set your manuscript aside for a while before proofing. Some distance from it will help you see mistakes more easily.

- Make a list of mistakes you need to watch for so you know what to look for. Eliminate unnecessary words before looking for mistakes.

- You can use both a printout and the computer to help catch errors. Reading out loud is helpful for spotting run-on sentences and other problems that you may not see when reading silently. Watch out for mistakes with homonyms (e.g., *they're, their, there*) and typos (e.g., *he* for *the*) that a computer spell checker may miss.

- To help keep you from skipping ahead of possible mistakes, use a blank sheet of paper to cover up the lines below the one you are reading.

- Use the computer's search function to find mistakes you're likely to make. For example, you can search for *it*, if you confuse *its* and *it's*. You may want to specify a search that includes a space before "it" (for example, " it" instead of "it") to eliminate instances where "it" could appear as part of a larger legitimate word, like "exit" or "legitimate" or "kittens". Search for *ing* if dangling modifiers are a problem. Also check for quotation marks or opening parentheses if you tend to leave out the closing ones.

- Check separately for each kind of error by following whatever technique works best for you to identify that kind of mistake. For example, read backwards, sentence by sentence (when you read backwards, you are forced to examine each sentence one at a time without context) or word by word to check for fragments. Read forward through again to be sure subjects and verbs agree. Then search for *this, it,* and *they* to trace pronouns to antecedents.

STEP 5 – FORMAT YOUR BOOK

EBOOK

Formatting eBooks is quite different from formatting print books. Since there are no "pages" in eBooks, page numbers are irrelevant. Most e-reading devices and e-reading applications allow the reader to customize how to display your book. As there are many different brands and models of e-readers on the market, your book will look different on every device. Anyone with an Internet connection can purchase and read your eBook on their phones, tablets, or reading devices immediately.

I formatted Jack's manuscript during the beta reading and editing processes because I liked it to always look nice and neat.

Unfortunately, editing and proofreading created some formatting issues, and I had to reformat everything again when I converted Jack's book into eBook format. In hindsight, I could have saved time if I had formatted the file as the last step before converting it to eBook format.

There are three methods to format your eBook:

Method 1   Format and lay out your book file using word processing software. Some distributors will convert your manuscript for you when you upload your book file to their website.

Method 2   Format and lay out your book file using word processing software, and then import it into a conversion software to convert the book file into different eBook formats.

Method 3   Use a writing/conversion software like Scrivener to write and convert your book file to different eBook formats.

For Jack's book, I used Method 1 and followed the Smashwords Style Guide to format my Microsoft Word file and publish an eBook on Smashwords and I used Calibre in Method 2 to convert the book file for other retailers.

3.15   What I learned about eBooks

- Amazon uses .mobi files and other retailers use .epub files. Other digital formats are Palm Doc (PDB), Portable Document Format (PDF), LRF, Rich Text Format (RTF), and HTML reader.

- Although eBook formats support images, they don't work well with books that have a lot of images. Your eBook will look different from a print book: Images may not appear in the exact position you intended, or the print-quality image that looks great on glossy paper may not look so great on a small black-and-white e-reading device.

- You will need to make extra effort to get special styling, tables, and columns to show properly.

- Your book's digital file size matters, because Amazon includes a delivery cost in their pricing setup that eats into your profit. Where possible, consider linking to images on your website or other websites like Pinterest. Some retailers may also have a file size limit.

- If you have both eBook and print book published and linked on Amazon, the eBook Print Length may be your print book's actual number of pages. Otherwise, it will be a system-generated number. You can contact KDP support to link all your books together.

- You can autograph your eBook for your readers through Authorgraph:

  (https://www.authorgraph.com/authors/becausenovel).

  Authorgraph is a personal, digital inscription service for eBooks. A reader can send a request to you, and you can write a custom message and draw your signature completely in the browser window using a mouse (or your finger if you use a tablet) to send back. The information is not inserted in the eBook, but rather it is kept in a separate document that allows a reader to create a "collection" where he/she can keep all of his/her Authorgraphs together.

3.16   What I learned about formatting an eBook

- You don't need to worry about choosing a font or font size for your eBook. If you decide to choose a font, sans serif fonts are good choices for eBooks because they are more legible. These fonts do not have details or small decorative flourishes on the ends of some of the strokes that make up letters and symbols. An example of a sans serif font would be Arial.

- You don't have to worry about hyphenation, how to handle widows and orphans, or following the different header or footer rules.

- You don't usually need to include the cover in the book file.

- You should not include links to affiliate marketing pages or links to different eBook retailers. You can create retailer-specific versions, or one with a link to a central place where you have all the buy links.

- You should not link to PDFs because not all e-reading devices can support PDF format.

3.17 Checklist for formatting an eBook

- ☐ Did I use 12-point font size for text and 14-point for headings?

- ☐ Do all my links work properly?

☐ Did I remove all unnecessary hidden spaces, line breaks, tabs, and bookmarks?

☐ Did I remove all headers and footers?

☐ Did I resize my images before inserting them into the document to a maximum of 500 pixels in width?

☐ Did I make sure my images are not floating?

☐ Did I compress my images to 96 dpi to save on file size and download time?

☐ Do all my quotations have the proper open and close marks?

☐ Are my chapter headings and subheadings consistent?

☐ Did I use consistent styling?

☐ Did I use either line indents at the beginning of a paragraph, or the block paragraph method, but not both?

☐ Did I include all the front and back matter?

Downloadable Item

3.17-Checklist for formatting an eBook

Log in: https://goo.gl/gb2ata or **Sign up:** https://goo.gl/XxrEro

3.18   What I learned about writing/conversion software

- You will need to convert your manuscript from your word processing software to .epub or .mobi formats for eBooks. You can choose from several free or paid writing and conversion software programs. Some are designed for specific operating systems or platforms.

- If you plan to create retailer-specific eBooks, you will need a separate file for each retailer. That means if you change something in your book, you'll need to update each individual retailer's file.

- You should clean up your book file prior to using conversion software. Cleanup includes things like deleting tabs and extra paragraph returns, replacing ellipses with periods spaced with non-breaking spaces, and optimizing images.

- You may need some basic knowledge of HTML to use certain software. You can learn more about HTML at https://www.w3schools.com/html/default.asp.

3.19   Links to eBook formatting guides

- Amazon's Guide

  http://kdp.amazon.com/help?topicId=A17W8UMoMM

  SQX6

- Guido Henkel eBook Formatting Guide

  http://guidohenkel.com/2010/12/take-pride-in-your-

  ebook-formatting

- Smashwords Style Guide

  https://www.smashwords.com/books/view/52

PRINT BOOK

Print-on-demand (POD) technology has changed the way print books are published. POD is quick, easy, and very affordable. When a customer orders your book from a retailer, one copy is printed and sent directly to the customer. There is no longer a need to print hundreds or thousands of copies and, therefore, no need for storage.

Regardless of how a book is printed, you still need to format your book for printing. Unlike an eBook, you can control the layout of a print book. Formatting a print book requires you to specify margins, spacing, headers, page numbers, and font style and size.

3.20   What I learned about print books

- Many POD distributors provide templates for you to use to create your manuscript file and cover. You may need to convert your manuscript file to a Portable Document Format (PDF).

- Most POD distributors offer a wide range of fee-based options, from cover design to editing services to marketing material.

- It is usually but not always free to set up your print book depending on the distributor you use.

- You will need a certain number of pages for a print book. It has to be thick enough to show the book's spine.

- You can publish a separate print book with large print on CreateSpace. The process is the same, except you will need to use at least a 16 point font size for your manuscript and make changes to your cover design file to accommodate the new number of pages. You will also need to use a different ISBN and indicate that it is a large print book in the description.

- Each retailer has different setups and options with comparative strengths and weaknesses.

- You can set up a print book with CreateSpace without publishing it. When you do that, you can order a print book to proofread or send out for advance reviews. If you publish your print book before your eBook on Amazon, reviews can be posted for the print version. Then, after you publish your eBook, you can contact Amazon author support to link the versions together. When you do that, the same reviews will appear on both the print and eBook product pages when you launch your eBook.

3.21   Self-assessment: Should I do print books?

☐ Do I want to use them as a marketing tool, for example, hosting a giveaway for interested readers?

☐ Do I want to get advance reviews from professional reviewers? Some will require a print book.

☐ Do I want to enter into contests for awards?

☐ Do I want to be able to physically autograph my book?

☐ Do I want to sell them in bookstores?

☐ Do I want to get them into libraries?

☐ Do I want to use them to increase my eBook sales by comparison pricing? The higher price of paperback makes an eBook look less expensive by comparison.

Downloadable Item

3.21-Self-assessment: Should I do print books?

Log in: https://goo.gl/gb2ata or **Sign up:** https://goo.gl/XxrEro

3.22 What I learned about formatting a print book

- You will need to format your print book based on the trim size you choose. Depending on the distributor/printer, you will have different options for the interior print (black & white or full colour), paper colour (cream or white), etc.

- Use a simple and consistent layout for your book. The simpler you can make it, the easier your life will be! Good design on the pages will also make your book easy on readers' eyes.

- Your font and text size need to be consistent, clear, and suitable for the type of book that you are writing. A decorative and unusual font may look great in a title, but it's usually not a good choice for the entire text.

- Serif fonts are good choices for print books. Serifs are semi-structural details or small decorative flourishes on the ends of some of the strokes that make up letters and symbols. An example would be Times New Roman.

- Use a 12-point typeface and aim for an average of 12 words per line for better readability than 11-point as often suggested.

- It is good practice to start a new page for each chapter so that even if you change the size of the page, your chapter headings will remain at the top.

- Always use the highest resolution images that you can to ensure that they come out looking sharp. Colour images, will cost substantially more to print than will black and white.

- If your book has hyperlinks to websites, type out complete website addresses accurately for readers to copy into their Internet browser.

3.23   Five steps to format a print book

Step 1   Decide on the physical size of your book. The most commonly used page dimensions for trade paperbacks are 6" x 9", 5 1/2" x 8 1/2", and 5" x 8". It is generally cheaper to print the larger size, as you can fit more text in fewer pages.

Step 2   Download the correct template based on the physical size of your book. You can access different templates from CreateSpace at https://www.createspace.com/Products/Book/InteriorPDF.jsp

Step 3   Copy and paste your manuscript into the template.

Step 4   Customize your layout with typeface, font size, and paragraph indentation, spacing, and styling. You can change other settings such as margins and gutter, but make sure that you follow each distributor's submission specifications before doing so. You can access IngramSpark's guide at http://www.ingramspark.com/hubfs/downloads

/file-creation-guide.pdf or CreateSpace's guide through the *CreateSpace Submission Specification* link from the link in Step 2.

Step 5   Save your file in .doc, .docx, .rtf, and PDF formats.

3.24   Checklist for formatting a print book

- ☐ Is my page size correct? Word processors usually default to A4 or US Letter size, which are not standard for book publishing.

- ☐ Are my margins correct?

- ☐ Are the fonts used appropriate for my type of book?

- ☐ Did I set my font size to 12-point?

- ☐ Did I fully justify the text between margins?

- ☐ Are all my paragraphs (optional for the first paragraph) indented consistently between .25" and .5"?

- ☐ Did I check and correct hyphens?

- ☐ Did I check and correct widow and orphan lines? Widows and orphans are words or short lines at the beginning or end of a paragraph, which are left dangling at the top or bottom of a column, separated from the rest of the paragraph.

☐ Are my running heads and/or footers consistent?

☐ Are my chapter titles and subheadings consistent?

☐ Did I start my first chapter on a right-side page?

☐ Did I start all my other chapters on a new page and about one-third of the way down the page?

☐ Did I stop the running heads on the first page of a new chapter?

☐ Is my page numbering correct with odd numbers on the right and even numbers on the left?

☐ Are certain pages completely blank?

☐ Did I include all the front and back matter?

Downloadable Item

3.24-Checklist for formatting a print book

Log in: https://goo.gl/gb2ata or **Sign up:** https://goo.gl/XxrEro

FRONT AND BACK MATTER

3.25   Front Matter

Front matter includes the information before your book begins. There is no set rule, but usually you would include the following information. In a print book, these pages do not include page numbers or headers.

- Book Title Page
- Copyright
- Library and Archives Canada / Bibliothèque et Archives Canada or Library of Congress Control Number (LCCN), which is a serially-based system of numbering cataloging records in the Library of Congress in the United States. Include something similar from your country if you have it.
- International Standard Book Number (ISBN)
- Disclaimer
- License Note
- Acknowledgements.

Some authors include a brief description of the book and summaries of other books. However, keep in mind that most retailers only make a small percentage of the book available as a free sample, so if your front matter is long, it might prevent readers from getting enough of a sample of your book.

3.26   Back Matter

Back matter includes the information after your book ends. Like the front matter, there is no set rule as to what to include, but usually the following information is covered. In a print book, these pages do not include page numbers or headers.

- Acknowledgements
- About the Author
- Provide a website address to an opt-in page on your website for readers to sign up for your mailing list
- A request for readers to leave a review and the website address
- Blurb of upcoming book if you have one.

STEP 6 – DESIGN YOUR BOOK COVER

Presenting your book with a well-designed cover has become increasingly important in a crowded digital market. A professional book cover is a key part of your marketing and branding. Many self-published authors believe that you will need an amazing cover in order to sell your book. The trouble is that no one can define what "amazing" is, as it is so very subjective. Something that appeals to some may not appeal to others. There is always someone who will disagree with you. I decided to design Jack's book cover myself. I had several ideas I wanted to incorporate and I had some experience with graphic design. I presented the finished product to several people and received responses ranging from "awful" to "amazing." In short, everyone's taste is different and you simply cannot please them all.

So what should you do if you choose to design your own cover? Instead of driving yourself crazy over the mixed response, use the checklist below to guide you through the process.

3.27   What I learned about cover design

- Unless you have the design skills, it's better to find someone skilled to create your cover design for you. You can buy eBook and print covers separately, but you may get a better deal if you get them created at the same time.

- If you use stock photography, there's a good chance that someone else has used or is going to use it. If you want to see if the image you plan to use is overused, you may do a reverse image search by downloading the thumbnail image from the website and uploading it to http://images.google.com.

- You will need separate covers for eBook and print versions: an eBook only needs a front cover, whereas a print book needs a wraparound cover with a front, spine, and back. The width of your printed book's spine depends on the number of pages. You can calculate the spine width of your book using the instructions at https://www.createspace.com/Products/Book/CoverPD F.jsp and generate and download a template for your book:

https://www.createspace.com/Help/Book/Artwork.do

or

https://myaccount.lightningsource.com/Portal/Tools/C overTemplateGenerator

- You need to allow a space for a barcode on the back cover of your print book. A barcode can include an ISBN and a price. If a barcode is not automatically inserted for you by the printer or distributor, you will need to place it on your back cover. If you make your own barcode (https://www.bookow.com/resources.php) and include a price, you will need to update the cover every time you want to change the price.

- You may need to create a different print cover for each different printer/distributor, depending on the size of the book you select and the thickness of paper they use.

- Some advertisers will not advertise books with controversial covers.

- Although you can always replace the cover in the hopes that it will improve sales, you might end up with different covers for the same book on different websites, which may be confusing to your readers.

3.28   What I learned about images

- Images are intellectual property and may not be free to use even when they are freely accessible on the Internet. When you or your designer use someone else's image, make sure you read and understand the licensing agreement before using it. If you need to get permission, contact the copyright owner and describe the permission you need and get it in writing.

- A license can be either exclusive or nonexclusive, and it is often limited to a particular use. Exclusive rights are not always available but if you get them, it means that only you are able to use the image for the duration of your license. As a licensee, you would want the license to be as broad as possible so that you could use it in print, eBook, website, promotional materials, etc.

- There are image banks and stock image companies that offer millions of images from artists who upload their work for sale. You can pay a fee to use an image and they will handle the licensing for you instead of having you deal directly with the artist or rights holder.

- RGB (Red, Green, and Blue) and CMYK (Cyan, Magenta, Yellow, and Key (Black)) are colour models. Most screens, such as computer, phone, and TV, use RGB images whereas most printers print in CMYK. It is not possible to display identical colours in RGB and CMYK. Save eBook covers in RGB and print book covers in CMYK.

3.29   Links for images

These websites offer stock images that you may want to use for your cover. Make sure you always check and understand the image's licensing terms before using it.

- http://4freephotos.com

- http://alegriphotos.com

- http://commons.wikimedia.org/wiki/main_page

- http://deathtothestockphoto.com

- https://designschool.canva.com/blog/free-stock-photos

- https://www.flickr.com

- http://www.freedigitalphotos.net

- http://www.freeimages.com

- http://getrefe.tumblr.com

- http://www.gratisography.com

- http://images.google.com/hosted/life

- http://imcreator.com/free

- http://jaymantri.com

- http://kaboompics.com

- http://magdeleine.co/browse

- http://morguefile.com/archive

- http://nos.twnsnd.co

- http://pdpics.com

- http://pdphoto.org

- http://photos-public-domain.com

- https://pexels.com

- http://picdrome.com

- http://picjumbo.com

- http://picography.co

- http://pixabay.com

- http://publicdomainarchive.com

- http://public-domain-photos.com

- http://raumrot.com

- https://stocksnap.io

- http://snapwiresnaps.tumblr.com

- http://unsplash.com

3.30   What I learned about fonts

- Every font or typeface comes with a license that grants the right to use it in a specific manner. Most of the typefaces in your computer or software come with a standard license that allows for printing. You will need to check individual licenses for the fonts you want to use in your book. Even a font labeled as "free" may not always be free if used commercially.

- Even if the fonts are owned by the same person or organization, they cannot be given away to others or shared among computers, unless the license specifically allows that.

3.31   Links for fonts

These websites offer fonts that you may want to use for your cover. Make sure you always check and understand the font's licensing terms before using it.

- http://www.dafont.com
- http://www.fontsquirrel.com
- http://www.myfonts.com

3.32   Checklist for cover design

☐ Did I get the proper licenses to use the images and fonts?

☐ Did I use appropriate images, fonts, and effects for the genre?

☐ Did I use high-quality images?

☐ Did I use a maximum of two typefaces (which I can vary by size and spacing) to avoid looking too cluttered?

☐ If I must use script and calligraphy typefaces, did I make sure they are not in all caps?

☐ Did I use proper spacing and alignment?

☐ Is everything on the cover legible when it's a thumbnail at 160 x 100 pixels?

☐ Does the cover have a good contrast with strong light-to-dark transitions and shadows?

☐ Do I have separate cover designs for eBook (RGB) and print (CMYK) versions?

☐ Is my eBook cover at least 1,400 pixels wide?

☐ Does my print cover have an ideal height/width ratio of 1.6 (2,560 pixels on the long side and 1,600 pixels on the short side)?

☐ Does my print cover have a 300 dpi resolution?

☐ Does my print cover include a place for a barcode at the back?

Downloadable Item

3.32-Checklist for cover design
Log in: https://goo.gl/gb2ata or **Sign up:** https://goo.gl/XxrEro

3.33   Links for cover designers

These websites offer design services where you can hire a designer to make a cover for you.

- https://99designs.ca

- https://www.crowdspring.com

- http://designcrowd.com

- https://www.fiverr.com/categories/graphics-design/ebook-covers

- http://killercovers.com

STEP 7 – PUBLISH YOUR BOOK

DISTRIBUTION

Once you are ready to publish, there are many online retailers where you can sell your book. You can upload your eBook directly to individual eBook retailers online or choose to distribute through an eBook aggregator (like a middleman). Likewise, you can sell your print book directly through online retailers and brick-and-mortar bookstores or use a distribution service. The basic process is simple: you provide some key information about your book, upload your book and cover files, then click submit. After a short review period, you will receive a notification that your book is published or that you need to correct something.

When we first published Jack's book, we sold the eBook exclusively through Amazon. After our three-month exclusive contract with Amazon expired, we published to other eBook retailers.

Although it was not difficult to publish on different retailers' platforms, I wish there were more consistencies between them. Each retailer has its own distinctive interface and terminology. For example, every retailer places books in different categories and uses its own system to classify them.

3.34 Amazon's KDP (Kindle Direct Publishing) Select

We chose Amazon, as it is the biggest online bookstore and its KDP Select (https://kdp.amazon.com/select) program offers features that allow first-time authors such as my husband to:

- Receive a share of the KDP Select Global Fund when customers read the books from Kindle Unlimited (KU) and the Kindle Owners' Lending Library (KOLL). The KDP Select Global Fund is a pot of money that gets divided proportionally amongst the authors who have had their books downloaded. Kindle Unlimited is a subscription program (think a Netflix for books) that allows readers to read as many books as they want for about $10 per month. The Kindle Owners' Lending Library is a collection of books that Amazon Prime members who own a Kindle can choose a book from each month with no due dates.

- Have access to two promotional tools: Kindle Countdown Deals (https://kdp.amazon.com/help?topicId=A3288N75MH1 4B8) allows authors to run limited-time discount promotions on their books available on Amazon.com and Amazon.co.uk. Customers can see the regular price and promotional price on the book's detail page, and a countdown clock showing how much time is left at the promotional price; and Free Book Promotion (https://kdp.amazon.com/help?topicId=A34IQ0W14Z KXM9), where readers can get a book for free for a limited time.

- Help readers discover one's books by making them available through KU in the U.S., U.K., Germany, Italy, Spain, France, Brazil, Mexico, Canada, India, Japan, and Australia; and the KOLL in the U.S, U.K., Germany, France, and Japan.

3.35   What I learned about KDP Select

- When you enroll in KDP Select, you are enrolled for 90 days and your book is automatically included in both KU and KOLL programs. You will get one combined payment for both. Your book will still be available for purchase in the Kindle Store, and you will continue to earn profit on sales.

- While your book is enrolled in KDP Select, you cannot distribute your book digitally anywhere else, including on your website, or other blogs, even if you do not charge a fee. However, you can continue to distribute your book in any format other than digital.

- You are eligible for royalty payment for pages an individual customer reads your book for the first time.

Amazon sets and announces the royalty rate per page read each month. A customer can read your book as many times as they like, but you only get royalty payment for the number of pages read the first time the customer reads them. It may take months for customers to read pages in your book, but no matter how long it takes, Amazon will still pay you once it happens. This is true even if your KDP Select enrollment period has expired, and you choose not to re-enroll.

- If you enroll your book in KDP Select, you're eligible for the KDP Select All-Star Bonus (https://kdp.amazon.com/help?topicId=A2X66QXB12 WV2). Anyone with titles in KDP Select—even a brand-new author—is eligible, provided that you claim your title on your Author Central Page (https://authorcentral.amazon.com/gp/help?ie=UTF8&t opicID=200777990). All-Star bonuses are awarded monthly to the top 100 ranked authors and titles. Authors who publish books together are considered a single "author" for the purposes of KDP All-Star bonuses. All-Star recipients are notified by email and are also eligible for All-Star badges on their book detail pages.

3.36   eBook retailers

You may want to experiment with KDP Select to determine the best path to success for your book, or you may decide to publish widely.

After our exclusive enrollment with Amazon's KDP Select ended, we signed up with other retailers—a few through direct contact and a few through other aggregators or distributors.

- Amazon

  http://kdp.amazon.com

- Nook - Barnes & Noble (not directly available to Canadian publishers)

  https://www.nookpress.com

- Google Play / Google Books (no longer accepts new publishers. Potentially available through certain aggregators/distributors)

  https://play.google.com/books/publish

- iBooks

  https://itunesconnect.apple.com/WebObjects/iTunesCo

  nnect.woa/wa/digitalContractsSignup?ccTypeId=13

- Kobo

  https://writinglife.kobobooks.com

3.37   POD book distributors

- BookBaby

  https://www.bookbaby.com

- Blurb

  http://www.blurb.com

- CreateSpace

  http://www.createspace.com (Amazon owned)

- IngramSpark

  http://www.ingramspark.com

- Kindle Direct Publishing (Amazon owned)

  https://kdp.amazon.com

- Lightning Source

  http://lightningsource.com

- Lulu

  http://www.lulu.com

- Vervanté

  http://www.vervante.com

3.38   Aggregators

An eBook aggregator distributes and sells your book to a wide range of online retailers. Aggregators collect a percentage of sales (around 15%) to provide you with wide distribution, as well as centralized accounting and payment services. Aggregators can save you a fair amount of time, especially when you wish to make a change, as you only need to format your book once and they will re-format for all the other devices and retailers for you. However, because you can upload only one file, most aggregators do not offer the ability to create retailer-specific eBooks with links to your book or books on other retailers. For example, you can't have a link pointing to the iBooks store included in the Amazon version and vice versa.

A book distributor sells your print book to both online booksellers and brick-and-mortar bookstores. Even though book aggregation is different from distribution, most people use 'distribution' as an umbrella term, especially when the company provides both services. For example, Smashwords provides eBook aggregation only, but IngramSpark provides both print and eBook distribution.

- Draft2Digital

  https://draft2digital.com

- Smashwords

  https://www.smashwords.com

- Pronoun.com

  http://www.pronoun.com

Retailers	eBook Aggregators		
	Draft2 Digital	Smash words	Pronoun
24 symbols	x		
Amazon			x
Baker-Taylor Axis360*		x	
Baker & Taylor Blio		x	

Retailers	eBook Aggregators		
	Draft2 Digital	Smash words	Pronoun
Barnes & Noble (Nook)	x	x	x
Bibliotheca CloudLibrary*		x	
Gardners Extended Retail		x	
Gardners Library*		x	
Google Play			x
iBooks	x	x	x
Kobo	x	x	x
Library Direct*		x	
Odilo*		x	
OverDrive*		x	
Page Foundry/Inktera	x	x	
Scribd	x	x	
txtr		x	
Tolino	x	x	
Yuzu		x	

"*Smashwords offers these channels for selling eBooks to public libraries. When a book is sold to a library through any of these channels, the library acquires the book permanently into its collection, and may check out each copy of the book it has acquired to one patron at a time, with no simultaneous checkouts. If you later remove your book from Smashwords, or opt out of library distribution, the library will still maintain the perpetual right to lend it out to patrons because they purchased the book, much in the same way that if you sell a print book to a library or an eBook through an eBook retailer, you cannot take it away after the fact. If a library requests to migrate their purchased titles from one library aggregator-operated checkout system to another, Smashwords will permit it on request" (quoted from Smashwords.com).

IngramSpark distributes eBooks to the largest number of retailers and is currently the only reliable print distribution channel that indie authors can use to reach brick-and-mortar stores.

Bookstores generally do not like to order books from Amazon's CreateSpace, even though they see them in the database. We used both CreateSpace and IngramSpark. There is no fee to set up a book on CreateSpace, but IngramSpark charges a $45 setup fee, which may be waived with an initial order of 50 books within 60 days of set up. Additionally, there is an annual fee of $12 per book per year, and a fee for each time you need to update your file.

Once you upload your book to a store, it will be there ready to earn you money until you remove it.

3.39   Printing services

If you want to order books for resale or a giveaway, you can order them through CreateSpace or from a local or overseas printing service. Printing services do not distribute your book to retailers; they only print and ship your books.

3.40   What I learned about printing services

- Printing services often require you to order a minimum number of copies. Some printing services offer special deals where they will print extra copies for orders over a certain number of copies. For example, if you order 100 copies, you will get 105 copies.

- Shipping and custom fees (if applicable when shipping overseas) are typically separate from printing costs.

- A printing service prints your books according to your instructions and your files. Once you approve a proof, you take all responsibility for any errors in it. It is better to order a physical copy than to view the proof online so you know the print quality you are getting.

- Printing services have non-negotiable deadlines, and you must adhere to them. There will be additional costs if you miss a deadline or ask for changes.

- You can pay extra to have your books printed and shipped faster.

3.41   Links to printing services

- http://bookprintondemand.com

- http://48hrbooks.com

- http://sheridanbooks.com

3.42   What I learned about distribution

- Specific promotional opportunities on some stores are available only if you publish directly with the retailers. By going through an aggregator, you may lose out on sales, discounts, or other promotional opportunities.

- Some stores, such as CreateSpace and Smashwords, offer the ability for authors to create custom coupon codes for readers, reviewers, or contest participants. You can set coupons to expire at a certain date for an amount or percentage off the retail price.

- You can choose more than one option for print books. For example, use CreateSpace (without expanded distribution) or KDP to publish your book on Amazon; use IngramSpark to distribute your book to bookstores and libraries through the Ingram catalog; and use printing services to buy copies for sale or to give away.

- It is important to price your print book properly so you can make a profit.

- Certain retailers will allow you to set up your book before publication three to 12 months in advance.

- Some retailers let you choose how much of your book can be downloaded as a free sample, while others will automatically select the percentage of your book (usually under 20%, including all front matter) that can be downloaded for free. On Amazon, your sample will show when you click the Look Inside link on the cover of your book.

- POD distributors offer a wide range of printing options: hardbacks, embossing, etc.

- KDP is now offering print books, but they do not yet provide author copies or expanded distribution like CreateSpace. You can order author copies at cost through CreateSpace to resell or give away.

- If you use IngramSpark and have provided any eBooks to Amazon in the past 12 months, IngramSpark will not be able to provide eBook distribution service to Amazon through its program.

- If you want to use IngramSpark and already have your eBook in the iBooks store, you will need to remove it prior to uploading the same book into IngramSpark. Any reviews or ratings you have will not transfer when your titles reappear in the iBooks store.

- If you want to use the same CreateSpace ISBN for a print book in IngramSpark, you will need to disable CreateSpace's expanded distribution option first.

BOOK DESCRIPTION/BLURB

A book description or blurb is basically a sales pitch meant to entice a reader to buy or download your book. A book blurb should be a fair representation of the style of the book; it should tempt the reader to want to know more without giving away too much. Writing a book blurb may sound easy, but in reality it is quite difficult to encapsulate an entire book in only a few words or paragraphs.

Here's an example of a short blurb for Jack's book:

> *The tragic accident on Mount Everest changes everything for Roberto Sanchez, a loving husband to Monique, and father to Jenny. Now facing the toughest climb of his life, Roberto is troubled by his own ideals and morals. While his family life tumbles through turbulent events, Jenny receives her father's private journal — the one he promised as her inheritance, once he was dead — it is a race against time for her to get to him…before it's too late.*

Here's an example of a long description for Jack's book:

> *Six months ago, Roberto Sanchez was climbing the world's highest mountain.*
>
> *Now, he can't walk.*
>
> *The tragic accident on Mount Everest changes everything for Roberto, a loving 48-year-old husband to Monique, and father to Jenny. As a professional mountain climber and motivational speaker, he had reached the summit of many mountains and helped others reach theirs. Now facing the toughest climb of his life, Roberto is troubled by his*

own ideals and morals. As his family life tumbles through turbulent events, he is no longer the giver of service but the recipient—a shift that infuses anger and pushes away the people he loves most.

When Roberto is first introduced, he's a surly, bitter shell of a man, unable to cope with the result of the horrible accident. His wife and daughter are at their wit's end, fearing that although Roberto has survived death, he remains stubbornly locked in the icy clutches of a life-sapping grief. Only when his journal is cracked open, and stories of his past encounters emerge, is Roberto's true identity revealed.

Inspired by real-life events, this is Roberto's story—a broken man's climb from the furthest depths of human grief to the heights of self-awareness and discovery. It is a story that plumbs the very depths of the human psyche, showing the options for triumph or torment in choices and perspectives open to us all.

3.43   What I learned about book description/blurb

- It's good to come up with various versions of blurbs to use for different purposes. At a minimum, create one short teaser (about 40 words) and a long book description (about 250 words).

- You can always change the blurb if you desire. If you have a print book cover that includes the blurb, you will need to change it too.

- You can include quotes from well-known authors, mention awards, or include a couple of positive reviews you've received.

- Some retailers' platforms allow HTML elements that you can use to make your book description stand out. An HTML element usually consists of a start tag and end tag, with the content inserted in between. Here are some basic HTML ones:

  - `<b>Bold text</b>`

  - `<br>`Use this if you want a line break (a new line) without starting a new paragraph. The `<br>` tag is an empty tag, which means that it has no end tag.

  - `<em>Emphasized text</em>`

  - `<h1>Heading 1 (biggest, most important)</h1>`

- <h2>Heading 2</h2>

- <h3>Heading 3</h3>

- <h4>Heading 4</h4>

- <h5>Heading 5</h5>

- <h6>Heading 6 (smallest, least important)</h6>

- <i>Italic text</i>

- <li>Each list item starts with the <li> tag and ends with </li>

- <ol>An ordered list starts with the <ol> tag and ends with </ol>

- <p>Defines a paragraph</p>

- <pre>Preformatted text</pre>

- <strike>Strikethrough text</strike>

- Important text

- _{Subscript text}

- ^{Superscript text}

- <u>Underline text</u>

- <ul>An unordered list starts with the <ul> tag and ends with </ul>

- Review the descriptions of the top ten best sellers in your category and try to model them.

- For fiction, while there's no perfect formula for writing the best blurb, there are some patterns worth taking note of: Introducing the reader to the protagonist in a way that creates intrigue without delving into all the assorted details, and referencing the central point of conflict without explaining how a resolution may come about. There are no set rules for writing a book blurb, but there are different "formulas." For a fictional book, the basic formula describes the hero, his desire, and the obstacle he must overcome.

- For nonfiction, focus on solving the problem that the reader has and leave them wanting more. Use the table of contents if that helps. Convince the reader that you are qualified to speak on the topic.

Downloadable Item

3.43-Blurb helper

Log in: https://goo.gl/gb2ata or **Sign up:** https://goo.gl/XxrEro

KEYWORDS AND CATEGORIES

Selecting the right categories and keywords for your book is essential.

To find a book, buyers will often search for keywords or browse through different categories. If your book is not on the first couple of pages of the search results, they will not know it exists, let alone buy it. The right categories and keywords will help readers find your book and, as a result, will increase your sales.

Amazon allows you to select up to two different categories and up to seven different keywords for your book. Each category or keyword gives you an opportunity to find readers, so you should use all of them. When I set up Jack's book, I had a difficult time picking out only two categories because the book fits in several places. At that point, I didn't fully understand how Amazon's keywords and categories worked. In Book 2 (http://www.because.zone/because-self-publishing-works), I cover some techniques I used to get his book in more than two categories and have it appear on the first page of many keyword searches. Using keywords and categories to help readers find your book is part of every successful marketing plan.

3.44   What I learned about keywords

- On Amazon, keywords are used to influence the search results.

- You can use the Amazon search bar to discover the words and phrases that people are searching for. When possible, consider including the keywords you found in your title, subtitle, and book description. For nonfiction, if it makes sense to do so, you may want to title your book to match the keywords that people search for.

- Amazon provides you with seven fields, each with up to 50 characters for you to enter your keywords or short phrases. You can combine keywords and keyword phrases in the most logical order. For example, I could combine two phrases into one field: *"how to write a book"* + *"book about self-publishing"* = *"how to write a book about self-publishing"*. The book then will show up on either search term.

- Your search results in Amazon will improve as you sell more books.

3.45   What I learned about categories

- You can choose between two and five categories depending on the platform/retailer you use. The aim is to be granular enough that your book can stand out, but not so deep down the hierarchy that no one shops there. You want to make sure you choose the categories that make sense and fit your book.

- When picking a category for your book, you don't have to select both the main and sub category. In fact, it is wiser to choose a specific or sub category that has the fewest books. For example, instead of picking Fiction then General, pick Fiction, Thrillers then General.

- There are a number of Amazon stores in different countries, but the categories you selected in the KDP Dashboard will not consistently apply to all of them.

- In order to have your book included in certain subcategories on Amazon.com and Amazon.uk, you will need to select a main category and add certain keywords. You can find more details at

https://kdp.amazon.com/help?topicId=A200PDGPEIQ
X41.

3.46   Links to sites for keywords research tools

- Google AdWords Keyword Planner Tool

  http://adwords.google.com/KeywordPlanner

- Keyword Eye

  http://keywordeye.com

- Ubersuggest

  https://ubersuggest.io

PRICING

We set Jack's print book at $18.99 and his eBook at $6.99 US
dollars after reviewing and considering similar books within the same
genre. We priced our eBook higher than the average price of $4.99
for self-published full-length novels, and in Book 2 I discuss why
higher pricing gave us a marketing advantage.

I had hoped that our set retail price would be consistent among
all retailers, but soon I discovered that each retailer would arbitrarily
adjust it. Even on Amazon, the price fluctuates all the time.

There is no restriction on how high you can price your book, but it may affect your royalty rate. For example, for eBooks on Amazon, the author earns 70% of the list price for prices between $2.99 and $9.99. For books priced below $2.99 or above $9.99 the author only receives 35%. The only way to know what works for you is to test different price points and track your results. Also, if you price your book too low, you may not be able to run attractive promotions. For example, a book discounted $0.99 from $3.99 will seem more attractive to readers than a book discounted to $0.99 from $1.99.

3.47   What I learned about pricing

- eBooks use the agency pricing model where the author uploads the book to a retailer (directly or through a service that handles the distribution) and sets the price for the book. The retailer pays the author only when the book is sold to the consumer. Agency pricing is based on a pre-agreed payment structure, usually a percentage of the final sale price. For a $2.99 book at 70%, the author would get $2.09.

- When pricing your eBook on Amazon between $2.99 and $9.99, be aware that Amazon charges a delivery fee based on your book's file size. You can find more details at https://kdp.amazon.com/help?topicId=A29FL26OKE7 R7B.

- Where selling books in foreign markets, it's better to manually change your prices into foreign currency than to use the retailer's auto-conversion tool.

- You can price your book at any amount, however, statistically $1.99 is not a recommended price and certain retailers require your price to end with .99. You can use Amazon's KDP Pricing Support (Beta) feature, which shows the relationship between price and past sales and author earnings for KDP books like yours, to help you price your book.

- Retailers may discount your book without consulting you. They may even sell your book at a loss. All retailers, except Google Play, will pay you based on the price you set.

- Google Play pays about 52% profit on sale, and if you publish on it, you need to calculate and price your book higher (25% or more) than other retailers. This is because Google Play sometimes will discount your book to be the lowest price on the market, which other retailers will price match. When this happens, your profit is based on the discounted price and not on the price you set.

- Some authors make their books permanently free (permafree) as a part of their marketing strategy to build readership. Often a permafree title is a loss leader for a series. A loss leader is a book sold at a loss to attract readers. If you are in Amazon's KDP Select program, you can use free days to make your book free temporarily but not permanently on Amazon. To make your book permanently free on Amazon, you will need to be out of KDP Select and distribute your book to other retailers. After setting your book to be free ($0) at other stores, you can wait or ask Amazon to price match. Another way is to not publish directly on Amazon but use Pronoun (http://www.pronoun.com) to distribute your book to Amazon instead.

- Because printing requires overhead costs, there is a minimum price at which you can price your print books. Print books use the wholesale pricing model where the retailer pays the author for the book, then sets the price to sell to the consumer. With wholesale pricing, the retailer purchases copies at a percentage of the list price. For example, for a print book with a list price of $15.99, the retailer would receive a 30% discount and the author would get $11.19. The price the retailer sells the book for has no bearing on the author's profit. The author will still get $11.19 whether the retailer sells the book at $12.99 or $9.99.

- Standard print wholesale rates are generally between 45-60%, while a short discount is commonly between 20-35% off the list price. Bookstores expect a 40-55% discount and the ability to return unsold books. CreateSpace offers short discounts and no ability to return unsold books, so if you wish to sell your book in bookstores, you will need to set up your book with IngramSpark.

- Expanded distribution is when you publish your book to other online retailers, bookstores, libraries, and academic institutions through a distributor. The author gets the profit on a sale after printing and distribution costs are deducted.

- It is important that you price your print book high enough so both you and the retailer can make a decent profit. For example, if you listed your book at $9.99 and the retailer paid $6.49 for it, the total cost will be $7.14 after adding 65 cents for overhead expenses. This would give the retailer a buffer of only $2.85 to play with ($9.99 - $7.14) whereas if the list price was $15.99, the retailer would have more opportunities to run sales and still make a profit on the book.

- Any additional charges that can affect the final price of your book, such as taxes and delivery, should be taken into consideration when looking at distribution options.

INTERNATIONAL STANDARD BOOK NUMBER (ISBN)

The purpose of the ISBN is to establish and identify one title or edition of a title from one specific publisher, allowing for more efficient marketing of products by booksellers, libraries, universities, wholesalers, and distributors.

There are over 160 ISBN agencies worldwide, and each ISBN agency is appointed as the exclusive agent responsible for assigning ISBNs to publishers residing in their country or geographic territory.

As Canadians, we are fortunate to be able to get ISBNs for free, as there is a fee in some other countries.

3.48   What I learned about ISBN

- You only need an ISBN number if you are planning on selling a printed book at retail (this includes Amazon.com and other online retailers). You do not need an ISBN if you are only publishing a book for family, friends, conferences, or direct-to-consumer distribution purposes.

You typically don't need an ISBN for an eBook, but some distributors may require one.

- An ISBN helps make your book more discoverable to readers and other book buyers (from libraries and bookstores) and gains a free inclusion in Books in Print (http://www.booksinprint.com), the world's largest catalog of books, which is licensed to all major search engines and thousands of bookstores and libraries.

- You will need to have your own ISBN if you want to be listed as the publisher. Owning your own ISBNs gives you the ability to control the bibliographic record for your book. You can use an ISBN provided by a distributor if you intend to publish only one book, have no interest in starting a publishing company, or are on a tight budget. Using a distributor's ISBN on your book doesn't mean giving up your ownership or copyright on your work.

- You should apply to the ISBN agency responsible for the country where you are based. You can search for yours at https://www.isbn-international.org/agencies.

- You will need to have a separate ISBN for each format (i.e. hardcover, paperbound, audiobook, eBook, a different language, etc.) and for each majorly revised edition.

- ISBNs are not transferrable, and an ISBN can never be reused once it is assigned. An ISBN is printed above the barcode on the lower portion of the back cover of a book and on the copyright page.

- If you publish your print book on different platforms for expanded distribution, you will need separate ISBNs.

- Since 2007, the official ISBN system changed from 10 digit numbers to 13. A 10-digit ISBN can be converted to a 13-digit number, but not by merely placing three digits in front of the 10-digit number. Instead, you can use the converter at http://www.isbn.org/ISBN_converter.

3.49   Links to sites for ISBNs

- Bowker (US)

  https://www.myidentifiers.com/get-your-isbn-now

- Canada

  http://www.bac-lac.gc.ca/eng/services/isbn-

  canada/Pages/isbn-canada.aspx

- Nielsen (UK)

  https://www.nielsenisbnstore.com/Home/Isbn

COPYRIGHT

While your original creative work is automatically protected
by copyright when you create it, it is a good idea to register your
copyright. You can use the certificate of registration in court as
evidence that you own the protected work.

3.50   What I learned about copyright

- There is nothing in copyright law that sets a fixed
  "allowance" of what you can reproduce from a copyright
  protected work. If you want to quote someone else's song
  lyrics, novel, article, poem, or other work, you should

always ask for permission and you may have to pay to use their work.

- Public domain refers to a previously copyright-protected work for which the copyright protection has expired or to a work voluntarily released into the public domain.

- Copyright laws vary from country to country. There is no such thing as international copyright law. You can find your country's Intellectual Property Office through the Directory of Intellectual Property Offices at http://www.wipo.int/directory/en/urls.jsp

DIGITAL RIGHTS MANAGEMENT (DRM)

Digital Rights Management uses special computer code to stop users from copying or changing an eBook. When you upload your file for publishing, certain retailers will ask whether you want to enable this feature. DRM cannot be undone once enabled. Since DRM is about restrictions more than rights, we did not choose DRM for Jack's book.

3.51   What I learned about DRM

- DRM will add an extra layer of protection to prevent unauthorized sharing of your copyrighted work; however, it will not stop all piracy, as there are illegitimate ways to remove the DRM.

- DRM can prevent readers from having access to the book they purchased through different devices. For instance, both Apple and Kobo support the .epub format, but they each use a different DRM system; therefore, an eBook bought through Apple's iBook store can't be read on a Kobo eReader. Similarly, Amazon's DRM-enabled eBooks can only be read on Amazon devices and apps.

4. WEBSITES

AUTHOR WEBSITE

Once you have your book published, you are done with the publishing process and you do not have to do anything else. However, having a website will give you a place to generate some pre-release excitement and to market your book as soon as it is released.

Your website is your home on the Internet. You can build your site using someone else's name and space for free, or get your own domain name and hosting space with a small investment.

If you want to have a long-term career as an author, you will need to invest time and money to establish your online presence. In

Book 2 (http://www.because.zone/because-self-publishing-works), I include many more details about building and maintaining an author website, as it will be a necessary part of your marketing strategy. Eventually, your website should give you a place to sell books, build your brand, increase readership, and connect with your readers.

I have been designing and coding websites for many years, but before I published Jack's book, I built his author website (http://www.because.zone) on a WordPress platform. Using a content management system like WordPress is easier and faster than coding from scratch and requires no programming knowledge. At first, the website contained only a single page, but it has evolved over time to its current form.

There are a lot of options available for building a website. It is possible to build and publish a basic one-page website in under an hour. It doesn't have to be difficult; you just need to know how and where to start.

If you decide to have a website at this point, consider having a web page that includes these sections at a minimum:

- **About:** Include your professional biography and a profile picture of yourself. It's good to come up with various versions of biography to use for different purposes:

    - **Extended** – for website, proposals, interviews and media kits.

    - **Medium** – for guest blogs and marketing materials.

    - **Brief** – for social media sites and back cover of your print book.

- **Book:** Include your book cover image and an up-to-date description of your book. After you've published, you can add positive praise that you received and links to the retailers that sell your book.

- **Contact:** Include your contact information and links to your social media profiles if you're active elsewhere (e.g., Twitter, Facebook).

Ideally, you would want to build your site prior to publishing your book. Building a website is also an efficient way to collect email addresses from your website visitors so that you can notify them when your book is released. A mailing list is especially helpful if you intend to produce more books later on.

In the future, you may want to consider adding different features to your website that allow you to sell your book directly to your readers, to create a members-only section, to run contests, and so on. In Book 2, I cover all these matters, including building a mailing list (which gives you another marketing option), in much greater detail.

4.1   What I learned about creating an author website

- A domain name is a name given to a website that people can access through an Internet browser by typing its name. It's like your address or phone number on the Internet. You can register for a domain name based on your name or your book, for example, *www.yourname.com* or *www.yourbook.com*, as long as it has not been taken. Registration is renewed on a yearly basis, but you may get a discount when you register for longer periods.

- A web hosting service provider supplies space for your files and settings that connect your website to the Internet. There are free and paid hosting service providers and when you choose to have your site on someone else's domain, you will have an address like *yourbook.myfreewebsite.com.* Usually a paid web hosting service will include an email service which you can use an email address typically in the form of *yourname@yourdomainname.com* to send and receive emails.

- Some web hosting services provide both domain name registration and web hosting, but it's wiser to register the domain name separately so you can change either domain registrar or hosting service without affecting the other.

- You need to read and understand the terms and conditions of your web hosting service provider.

- Web hosting services have different plans, and some offer incentives such as free domain registration for a year or free advertising credits. There are often discounts for longer-term contracts.

- Select a web hosting service provider that provides the website-building platform that you want. Many authors choose WordPress (https://wordpress.org), as it is free and has many features.

- You can start building your mailing list by using Mailchimp's (http://mailchimp.com) free service that allows you to collect up to 2,000 email addresses for free. It is a good idea to build your mailing list now especially if you intend to write more books or want to connect with your potential ideal readers.

4.2   Five steps to creating your author website

Step 1   Register a domain name with a domain registrar such as https://www.namecheap.com. This step is optional if you are going to build your site on a free hosting platform (see Step 2 below).

Step 2   Choose a web hosting service that provides the website-building platform you want. There are free web hosting services such as http://www.wix.com, https://www.weebly.com and https://www.wordpress.com. You can follow your service provider's instructions on how to direct web traffic to your domain name through DNS (Domain Name Service).

Step 3   Install a website-building platform (a platform for building websites and managing your own online content).

Step 4   Configure the website-building platform. This includes installing and configuring the look and functions of your website.

Step 5   Create your content.

4.3   Links for web hosting services

- 1 & 1 Web Hosting

  https://www.1and1.ca/

- Bluehost

  https://www.bluehost.com/

- DreamHost

  https://www.dreamhost.com/

- GoDaddy

  https://www.godaddy.com

- HostGator

  http://www.hostgator.com/

- In Motion Hosting

  http://www.inmotionhosting.com/

4.4   Links for free website-building platforms

- Drupal

  https://www.drupal.org/

- Joomla

  https://www.joomla.com/

- WordPress

  https://wordpress.org/

4.5   Links for website-building tutorials

- SiteGround – How to Use Drupal

  https://www.siteground.com/tutorials/drupal/

- SiteGround – Joomla How-Tos for Beginners

  https://www.siteground.com/tutorials/joomla/

- SiteGround – WordPress How-To For Beginners

  https://www.siteground.com/tutorials/wordpress/

4.6   Checklist for building an author website

☐ Do I have an email address?

☐ Do I have my PayPal email/password or credit card information? I will need this for billing purposes.

☐ Do I have a list of domain names I want to search for?

☐ Do I have a username and password I am going to use?

☐ Do I have my biography?

☐ Do I have my author picture?

☐ Do I have my book cover?

- ☐ Do I have my book description?

- ☐ Do I have all my contact information, including links to social media profiles/sites?

- ☐ Do I have anything else I want to put on my author website?

Downloadable Item

4.6-Checklist for building an author website

Log in: https://goo.gl/gb2ata or **Sign up:** https://goo.gl/XxrEro

AMAZON AUTHOR CENTRAL

Besides your website, you may also want to create an Author Page on Amazon through Amazon Author Central. You can find more information about Amazon Author Central at https://authorcentral.amazon.com/gp/help?ie=UTF8&topicID=20 0497410.

The Author Page provides a handy place for customers to learn about you and your books, like getting your own free homepage on Amazon.

You can see Jack's Author Page at https://www.amazon.com/Jack-A.-Langedijk/e/B00NJD65YK.

You can share the most up-to-date information about yourself and your works with readers by adding your biography, photos, blog, video, Twitter feeds, and tour events to the Author Page.

4.7   What I learned about Amazon Author Central

- After you've signed in, you can search for your book(s) by title or ISBN. The book you select must be available for purchase on the Amazon.com website, and once selected, an account will be created.

- You may need to input your biography or photos manually. Check and see what shows up, and then add anything that is missing.

- You can see how your book and author ranks trend over time.

- You can make changes to your editorial review and book description sections. Changes you make through Author Central will appear on your product detail page quicker than when you make the changes through the KDP Dashboard. However, if you subsequently make changes through the KDP Dashboard, KDP changes will override the changes you made in Author Central.

- Author Central is only available for the following countries, and the features are not the same for all the sites. Once you set up Author Central in the US, it automatically propagates your Author Central page for Amazon India (Amazon.in):

  - France (Amazon.fr)

    https://authorcentral.amazon.fr

  - Germany (Amazon.de)

    http://authorcentral.amazon.de

  - Japan (Amazon.co.jp)

    https://authorcentral.amazon.co.jp

  - United Kingdom (Amazon.co.uk)

    https://authorcentral.amazon.co.uk

  - United States (Amazon.com)

    https://authorcentral.amazon.com

- Works written in English will show up under foreign authors in France, Germany, and Japan sites.

GOODREADS

You may also want to set up your profile on Goodreads (https://www.goodreads.com). It's another place to advertise you and your book to millions of readers.

4.8   What I learned about Goodreads

- After you register for an account, you will want to apply for a Goodreads Author upgrade. Once your account is upgraded, you can join the Goodreads Author program and add all your contact details. You may add photos, videos, your bio, your book(s), and you can upload your eBooks and add friends. You can also link your blog posts (if you have any) to your Goodreads page so that readers can read them from your Goodreads page without having to visit your blog. Here's Jack's Goodreads   page: https://www.goodreads.com/author/show/8379789.Jac k_A_Langedijk

- You can upload samples of your books in PDF and .epub formats.

- You can run promotions and contests to give free copies of your print books to readers and hope to receive reviews on both Goodreads and Amazon. Readers' ratings and reviews of your book appear on your Goodreads page. There is a cost for running a giveaway for eBooks, but it is free for print book giveaways.

- You can interact with readers through private messaging or through different groups https://www.goodreads.com/group.

5. PUBLISHING CHECKLISTS

The following checklist lists items that you may want or need to do, get, or complete before you publish your book.

5.1 PRE-PUBLISHING

☐ Do I want to send advance review copies four to six months before publication? This is important if I want to include reviews on my print book cover design or have them ready when I publish.

☐ Do I have an email address?

☐ Do I have my tax identification information (ie. SIN, EIN, TIN) ready? (Non-US citizens will need to complete a tax form in order to avoid a 30% withholding tax.)

☐ Do I want to register my company as the publisher/imprint name?

☐ Do I need ISBNs? This may be optional for eBooks depending on retailers.

☐ Do I have my banking details or a PayPal account?

☐ Do I want to apply for a copyright certificate?

☐ Do I want to build an author website?

☐ Do I want to set up profiles on social media networks (Facebook Page, Twitter, Tumblr, etc.)?

☐ Do I want to get my Cataloguing in Publication (CIP) information if I intend to publish more than 100 print copies? (applies to Canadian authors only)

5.2   PUBLISHING

Before creating an account on the various retailers, gather the following information in one place so you have it ready. By now, it shouldn't take too long to finally get your book out into the world!

☐ Do I have a list of retailers/distributors I want to use?

☐ Do I have a title (and subtitle) for my book? Although titles can be changed later, it is not easy to do. Avoid using special characters or long titles as some retailers may not be able to accommodate them. You can use a tool at http://www.lulu.com/titlescorer/index.php to check whether or not you've got a killer title.

- ☐ Do I have my book description/blurb?
- ☐ Do I have all the positive reviews I received for my book?
- ☐ Do I have the name(s) and role(s) of the contributors I want to add?
- ☐ Do I have the name that I would use as the publisher?
- ☐ Do I have my ISBNs?
- ☐ Do I have the list of up to five categories I want to list my book under? Amazon allows two categories and other retailers may allow more.
- ☐ Do I have the list of up to seven keywords I want to use?
- ☐ Have I decided on the list prices for my eBook and print book?
- ☐ Do I have a picture of myself for my author profile?
- ☐ Do I have a biography written in third person?
- ☐ Do I have my tax identification information?
- ☐ Do I have my manuscript in the proper layout and formats (.epub, .mobi, .docx, .doc, .rtf, PDF)?

☐ Do I have my different book cover files in the proper format and resolution for eBook and/or print? Are my title (and subtitle) and author name on the cover? For print book cover, is the barcode with a correct ISBN in the proper location?

☐ Have I used the online previewer (if one is provided) to review the proof before publishing?

5.3   POST-PUBLISHING

After you finish publishing your book, you still have work to do. You can use this checklist to remind yourself which tasks remain after publication.

☐ Did I buy a copy of my book from the retailer to check if everything looks okay?

☐ Did I check the Look Inside sample of my book (all formats) on Amazon to make sure only a limited sample is shown?

☐ Did I claim my book on all Amazon Author Central websites?

☐ Did I add my book to Goodreads?

☐ Did I add the buy links to my website and social media profiles?

☐ Did I add the links to my public social media profiles such as Facebook author page, Twitter, Goodreads, etc. to my website?

☐ Did I send copies of my book to Legal Deposit? (applies to Canadian authors only)

Downloadable Item

5.3-Publishing checklists

Log in: https://goo.gl/gb2ata or **Sign up:** https://goo.gl/XxrEro

6. SALES & EARNINGS REPORTS

The following table shows the approximate profit percentages for each distributor. Before publishing, please check their websites for the most current rates, terms, and conditions.

Retailer/Distributor	Your Profit Percentage
Amazon	35% – 70% depending on the price of the book
CreateSpace	20% – 60% of net profit
Draft2Digital	60% – 85%
Google Play	52% based on converted price from US$

Retailer/Distributor	Your Profit Percentage
iBooks	70%
IngramSpark	45% – 60% of net profit
Kobo	70%
Lulu	80% – 90% of net profit
Nook	60%
Pronoun	70%
Smashwords	60% – 85%

6.1 What I learned about sales and earnings

- Most distributors pay monthly, 60 days after the end of the month of sales. Some pay quarterly, and some pay when a minimum amount is reached.

- Generally, you can choose which currency you wish to receive your profit. You will need to provide either your banking details for direct bank deposit or an email address that is associated with a PayPal account.

- You will also need to complete tax information. Non-US citizens may want to complete an additional form to avoid having 30% of their earnings withheld in anticipation of taxes owed.

- You can see and download reports of your book sales and earnings at any time.

7. EQUIPMENT & TOOLS

You will need to have access to a computer with Internet connection plus some of the following tools/software.

Word Processing – Free

LibreOffice https://www.libreoffice.org

OpenOffice Writer http://www.openoffice.org

Word Processing – Paid

Microsoft Word https://products.office.com/en-ca/word

Email Client – Free

Gmail http://www.gmail.com

Hotmail http://www.hotmail.com

Email Client – Paid

Microsoft Outlook

https://products.office.com/en-ca/outlook/email-and-calendar-software-microsoft-outlook

Images Compression – Free

Compressor http://compressor.io

Cover Creator – Free

Amazon Kindle Cover Creator

http://kdp.amazon.com/help?topicId=A36JL6A6XSO6VH

CreateSpace Cover Creator

https://www.createspace.com/Help/Book/Artwork.do

Photo Editing – Free

https://www.canva.com

https://www.gimp.org

http://imagebatch.org

http://www.photobucket.com

https://pixlr.com

http://pizap.com

Photo Editing – Paid

Adobe PhotoShop http://www.photoshop.com

eBook Converter – Free

Calibre https://calibre-ebook.com

iBook Author http://www.apple.com/ca/ibooks-author

Online eBook Converter http://ebook.online-convert.com

Sigil https://sigil.en.softonic.com

Zinepal http://zinepal.com

eBook Converter – Paid

Creatavist https://atavist.com

Jutoh http://www.jutoh.com

Vellum https://vellum.pub (for MAC computers)

Word to HTML Converter – Free

Word to Html http://wordtohtml.net

PDF Converter – Free

PDF995.com http://pdf995.com

Writing Organizer & Converter – Paid

PerfectIt Pro http://www.intelligentediting.com

Scrivener https://www.literatureandlatte.com/scrivener.php

Voice Dictation – Free

Google Docs https://docs.google.com

Create new document then select Tools, Voice typing…

Voice Dictation – Paid

Dragon NaturallySpeaking

http://www.nuance.com/dragon/index.htm

8. PUBLISHING COSTS

These are one-time estimated costs in US dollars:

Service	Cost Range
Website design	$0 to $2,000+ depending on features
Beta Reader	Free to $0.003 per word
Editing	Developmental $0.01 to $0.05 per word
	Line $0.006 to $0.036 per word
	Copy $0.003 to $0.009 per word
Formatting	$50 to $200
Cover design	$50 to $500

Service	Cost Range
Publishing	Free for eBooks to $49 for a print book on IngramSpark
ISBN	Free to $150 depending on the country you live in
Copyright	Under $50

These are potential ongoing estimated costs in US dollars:

Service	Cost Range
Website domain name registration	$10 to $15/year
Website hosting	Free to $15/month
Publishing	$12/year for print books on IngramSpark

These are optional estimated costs in US dollars:

Service	Cost Range
Writing and Conversion Software	Free to $200

Service	Cost Range
Photo Editing Software	Free to $700
Website design	Free to $100 for a basic website

9. MISCELLANEOUS

WORKING WITH OTHERS

As I mentioned before, you can do everything yourself if you have the skills, time, and desire, though you may need to learn a few new skills. Sometimes, though, you may be better off outsourcing jobs to a professional. If you decide to outsource anything, these tips will help make working with others more pleasant and your investment more worthwhile.

- Respect the instructions and guidelines of others.
- Spend time finding out how others complete their task.
- Be clear with your requests, expectations, and correspondence.

- Ask questions, but don't ask for anything that you don't want.

- If you ask for something and get something different in return, be honest with your objections and criticisms.

- Deal with conflicts in private. When they arise, stay calm, explain the issues clearly, and propose workable solutions.

- Return messages and emails within two days, even if it is just an acknowledgement.

- Respect everything mutually agreed upon such as timelines, budget, and payment schedules.

- Be agreeable as you decide upon reasonable prices, reasonable timelines, and reasonable terms and conditions.

Downloadable Item

GS1-Service Providers

Log in: https://goo.gl/gb2ata or **Sign up:** https://goo.gl/XxrEro

CATALOGUING IN PUBLICATION (CIP)

CANADIAN AUTHORS

Cataloguing in Publication (CIP) is a voluntary program of cooperation between publishers and libraries, coordinated by Library and Archives Canada. It enables the cataloguing of books before they are published, and allows for the prompt distribution of cataloguing information to booksellers and libraries.

The CIP entry for Jack's book looks like this:

Library and Archives Canada Cataloguing in Publication

Langedijk, Jack A., author

Because / Jack A. Langedijk.

Issued in print and electronic formats.

ISBN 978-0-9937586-1-4 (paperback).

--ISBN 978-0-9937586-0-7 (ebook)

I. Title.

PS8623.A63B43 2015   C813'.6   C2015-908315-X

C2015-908316-8

9.1 What I learned about CIP

- To be eligible for CIP, a publication must have a print run of more than 100 copies.

- Library and Archives Canada creates separate records for print, electronic, audio, and other formats in their database, but they will not send you separate CIP data for each format. You will have one CIP book entry containing the ISBNs for all the formats of a particular title. This book entry is intended for inclusion in all formats of your publication.

- You need to include the CIP data on the verso (left-side page) without alterations made to sequence, punctuation, capitalization, or format.

9.2 List of steps to get your CIP

Step 1 Follow the instructions and complete a CIP application form at http://www.bac-lac.gc.ca/eng/services/cip/Pages/application-forms.aspx.

Step 2 After receiving your CIP details through email, insert the information as is on the left-side page after the title page or the copyright page of your print book. You may also include it with the eBook format if you wish.

US AUTHORS

Please check out the Cataloging in Publication Program at https://www.loc.gov/publish/cip

LEGAL DEPOSIT REQUIREMENT FOR CANADIAN PUBLISHERS

All Canadian publishers are required to deposit copies of their work into the national library collection for public consultation and use as stipulated by the Library and Archives of Canada Act (http://laws-lois.justice.gc.ca/eng/acts/L-7.7/). Legal deposit applies to all publications produced in Canada and all mediums and formats.

Titles by Canadian authors published outside of Canada are not subject to legal deposit; however, they are welcome to donate copies of their work to the collection.

Legal deposit applies to publications including but not limited to:

- Books (monographs)
- Serials (journals, periodicals, magazines)
- Sound, video and spoken-word recordings

- Multimedia or instructional kits

- CDs and DVD-ROMs

- Microforms

- Cartographic materials

- Online or digital publications

Legal deposit does not apply to the following:

- Official publications of Canadian provincial, territorial, and municipal governments

- Loose-leaf publications with updates in print format

- Materials not intended for public sale or distribution

- Pre-publication manuscripts or materials not formally published

- Portions of publications (abstracts, summaries, table of contents) without the complete text

- Publications missing essential attributes (a distinct title, a specific author or authoring body, a specific publication date, etc.)

- Materials with little or no substantial text (stationery, agendas, notebooks, forms, calendars, postcards, posters, newsletters, alerts, bulletins, documents composed only of hyperlinks, etc.)

- Materials in poor physical condition.

9.3   Links for Legal Deposit

- Additional examples and information

  http://laws-lois.justice.gc.ca/eng/regulations/SOR-2006-337/index.html

- Deposit of Physical or Analogue Publications

  http://www.bac-lac.gc.ca/eng/services/legal-deposit/Pages/physical-analogue.aspx

- Deposit of Online or Digital Publications

  http://www.bac-lac.gc.ca/eng/services/legal-deposit/Pages/online-digital-publications.aspx

USEFUL LINKS

FILE STORAGE AND SHARING

- Amazon S3 http://aws.amazon.com – Provides secure and highly scalable space for storing and retrieving data from anywhere.

- Dropbox http://dropbox.com – Provides storage for files that can be shared and viewed on any device.

- Google Drive http://drive.google.com – Provides storage for files that can be shared.

- OneDrive http://onedrive.live.com – Provides storage for files that can be accessed on phone, tablet, or computer.

FREELANCE MARKETPLACES

You can use these sites to find people to provide services you need, such as editors, graphic designers, and virtual administrators.

- Fiverr http://fiverr.com – Providers offer services starting from a rate of $5.

- Freelancer http://freelancer.com – Providers of various project terms and sizes based on a bidding system.

- Guru http://guru.com – Providers offer work in technology, creative arts, and business.

- Reedsy http://reedsy.com – Providers offer publishing services.

- Upwork http://upwork.com – Providers offer short and long term work with different levels of skillsets.

IDEA GENERATORS

- ContentIdeator   http://contentforest.com/ideator – Creates titles for any keyword you provide.

- Hubspot's   Blog   Topic   Generator http://hubspot.com/blog-topic-generator – Generates relevant blog post titles based on terms that you provide.

- Name Generator http://namegenerator.biz/pseudonym-generator.php – Randomly generates both male and female names.

LINK SHORTENERS, BACKLINKS AND UNIVERSAL LINKS

- Bit.ly http://bit.ly – Provides URL shortening and bookmarking service.

- Book Linker http://booklinker.net – Provides global universal link that automatically takes readers to your book in the correct Amazon store.

- Goo.gl http://goo.gl – Provides URL shortening service.

MONITORING TOOLS

- Google Alerts http://google.com/alerts – Monitors and sends e-mail updates on the topics you choose, for example, when someone mentions your name or your book.

- Mention http://mention.com – Tracks and sends alerts of a mention of the topics you follow.

- Tagboard http://tagboard.com – Monitors keywords on multiple social media platforms and creates a customized board that shows your chosen keywords.

- Yasiv http://yasiv.com – Displays a visual map of your book in connection with the also-bought lists attached to other Amazon books.

PLAGIARISM CHECKERS

- Anti-Plagiarism http://sourceforge.net/projects/antiplagiarismc – Software designed to detect plagiarism.

- CopyScape http://copyscape.com – Online software that scans the Internet for copies of work.

- PaperRater http://paperrater.com – Offers grammar checking, plagiarism detection, and writing suggestions tools.

- Plagiarism http://plagiarisma.net – Provides online search and software downloads that detect plagiarism for various types of files.

PRODUCTIVITY TOOLS

- Bubble http://bubbl.us – Lets you create mind maps.

- SimpleMind http://simpleapps.eu/simplemind/ Allows you to create and organize your map on your phone or tablet.

- Google Keep http://google.com/keep – Keeps lists, pictures, and notes synced across all your devices.

- Todoist http://en.todoist.com – Task management software that facilitates collaboration.

- Xmind http://xmind.net – An open-source mind maps app.

REFERENCE TOOLS

- Reference http://reference.com – Online encyclopedia, dictionary, and thesaurus.

- Wikipedia http://wikipedia.org – Reference website that covers millions of topics in different languages.

- Local libraries may have databases that provide different types of reference materials.

RESEARCH TOOLS

- Aaron Shepard's Sales Rank Express http://salesrankexpress.com – Checks Amazon sales ranks for books.

- eReaderIQ http://ereaderiq.com – Tracks Kindle books' prices.

- KD Pulse http://kdpulse.com – Compares and tracks books.

- KDSpy http://kdspy.com – Analyzes Amazon marketplace and reveals niches.

- KeywordInspector http://keywordinspector.com – Tools to help you optimize your sales on Amazon.

- KindlePreneur Sales Rank Calculator https://kindlepreneur.com/amazon-kdp-sales-rank-calculator/ – Calculates daily sales number and seller's rank on Amazon.

- K-Lytics http://k-lytics.com – Online tool for instant market data trends on Amazon.

- MerchantWords http://merchantwords.com – Database of most commonly searched words and phrases on Amazon.

- NovelRank http://novelrank.com – Tracks book sales and ranks on Amazon.

TRACKING AND TESTING RESOURCES

- Facebook Insights http://facebook.com/insights – Helps you get an idea of how well your page is performing.

- Google Analytics http://google.com/analytics – Helps you get information about website traffic.

- Pinterest Analytics http://analytics.pinterest.com – Helps you understand how users engage with your content.

- QuantCast http://quantcast.com – Provides the data you need to know your audience.

- Twitter Analytics http://analytics.twitter.com – Helps you measure engagement and learn how to make your Tweets more successful.

VALIDATOR

- .epub Validator http://validator.idpf.org – A tool that recognizes many types of errors in .epub files.

WORD COUNTER

- AnyCount http://anycount.com – Produces automatic word, character, line, and page counts for all common file formats.

- CharacterCount   http://charactercountonline.com – Online character- and word-counting tool.

- WordCounter http://wordcounter.net – Counts number of characters and words in text.

ALL THE BEST WITH YOUR PUBLISHING JOURNEY

By now you have probably come to the conclusion that there is often more than one way to do something and that you can always start and learn something new. I hope I've given you the benefit of my experience so that you have the knowledge and confidence you need to pursue your goal.

I have created a section on our website that contains tools, checklists, and templates, in addition to all those listed throughout this book. As my valued reader, you can sign up at http://www.because.zone/join-us/bspw1-reg to gain immediate access. By signing up, you will also be notified of my future special offers, including Book 2 (http://www.because.zone/because-self-publishing-works) in the *Because Self-Publishing Works* series, where I share my learning and experience in marketing Jack's book.

I would appreciate it if you'd post a short review for this book. Your review will help other readers know what to expect and help them decide whether this book would be of use to them. It will also help me to continuously make improvements based on your comments and suggestions. Would you please take a few seconds to let your social networking friends know about this book if you think they would benefit from it? Thank you.

Please feel free to reach out to me at vvcam@because.zone if I can be of further assistance to you in any way.

There is no better or perfect time to start your self-publishing journey. I am cheering you on as you learn and progress one step at a time towards your publishing goal.

Blessings to you!

V.

ACKNOWLEDGEMENTS

To my daughter, Candace, thank you for being my alpha reader and making our beta readers' and editors' jobs much easier. You never cease to amaze me each and every day. I am so incredibly grateful to have a daughter who is also my best friend.

To my wonderful Quiethouse Editing team of beta readers, Colleen Alles and Lena Hillbrand, thank you for your thoughtful comments and suggestions. Your kind words and gentle steering helped me so much. Thank you, Starr Waddell, for your consistent professional and friendly service that I can continuously count on.

To my amazing editors, David Loving from davidaloving.com and Tom Shutt from mainlineediting.com, thank you so much for making every word shine.

To my great friends, Gail and Loraine, whose endless support means the world to me—thank you for always being there.

Many huge thanks to all of the loyal supporters of *because*. Your constant presence and feedback helped make *because* the success that it is. And thanks to all of you for the motivation and support to create the books in this series.

And to my darling, Jack, thank you for being the best man on planet Earth. Your love and support helped me to believe I can fly.

ABOUT THE AUTHOR

V.V. Cam's philosophy of life exemplifies the saying "Give a man a fish, and you feed him for a day. Teach a man to fish, and you feed him for a lifetime." When it comes to exploring the ever-changing world of self-publishing, V.V. has proven she is no stranger to embracing new worlds and ideas. She has not only learned how to fish, but also has spent her life teaching hundreds of others to become self-reliant.

V.V. and her family had to flee Vietnam by boat when she was just at the tender age of 13. When most young girls at that age would have been worrying about acne and boys, she was living in Hong Kong, housed in a prison that had been turned into an overcrowded refugee camp.

That was where she started her journey to become the happy and successful wife, mother, and entrepreneur that she is today. While working in an electronics factory earning money to help her family survive the hardships of daily life, she taught herself to read and write Chinese. A year later, a church sponsored her family to start their new life in a small town in Ontario, Canada.

She put her language learning skills to use again, this time mastering English. She soon became one of the top students at her school and helped the office staff with her typing and office skills. Along with her industrious family, she learned to sew and made money sewing for local shops and for friends.

Her resume soon included an impressive list of accomplishments: She worked her way from seamstress, waitress, bartender, and receptionist to IT support specialist and trainer, to real estate agent and broker. She has worked in executive positions with large organizations managing finances, human resources, and relationships and has built a couple of small businesses.

In her spare time, she created two high-traffic and successful websites that offer teaching tools and support to the Vietnamese communities. She's also founded a philanthropic organization that provides micro loans for poor people in Vietnam.

The two books in the *Because Self-Publishing Works* series share the knowledge she learned while helping her husband publish and market his book. You will appreciate her pragmatic advice, compassionate voice, and succinct writing style that bring clarity and fresh perspective to the evolving self-publishing industry.
www.because.zone/because-self-publishing-works

INDEX

account, 123, 125, 128, 133

acknowledgement, 31, 143

Acknowledgements, 66, 67

advance, 8, 14, 32, 60, 92, 127

advertise, 71, 125

advertising, 9, 118

aggregator, 78, 85, 88, 91

alerts, 148, 150, 151

Amazon, 1, 4, 14, 53, 54, 58, 60, 79, 80, 82, 83, 84, 85, 86, 89, 91, 92, 99, 100, 101, 102, 103, 104, 105, 108, 113, 122, 123, 124, 126, 129, 130, 132, 136, 148, 150, 151, 153, 154

antecedents, 50

author, i, 7, 8, 9, 13, 14, 22, 23, 60, 82, 92, 103, 104, 106, 107, 114, 115, 117, 119, 121, 122, 123, 125, 128, 129, 130, 131, 137, 144, 147

Author Central, 82, 122, 123, 124, 130

autograph, 54, 60

backups, 42

banking, 128, 133

barcode, 70, 76, 110, 130

beta readers, 18, 29, 30, 31, 33, 35, 48

biography, 116, 121, 123, 129

blog, 73, 123, 125, 150

blurb, 9, 84, 93, 94, 95, 96, 98, 129

Blurb, 67, 84, 93, 98

booksellers, 10, 85, 108, 144

bookstore, 24, 40, 79

bookstores, 15, 60, 78, 85, 91, 107, 109

brand, 21, 82, 115

budget, 16, 109, 143

build, 23, 105, 114, 115, 116, 119, 128

business, 4, 9, 10, 11, 12, 13, 15, 17, 22, 40, 43, 149

Canada, 66, 81, 111, 144, 145, 146, 159

Canadian, 44, 83, 128, 131, 144, 146, 147

career, 22, 114

cataloging, 66

Cataloguing, 128, 144

categories, 1, 77, 79, 99, 101, 129

category, 98, 99, 101

certificate, 111, 128

chapter, 33, 38, 39, 43, 56, 62, 65

characters, 29, 33, 34, 41, 100, 128, 155

checklist, 69, 127, 130

coding, 115

colour, 61, 72

commitment, 20, 30

communicating, 17, 45

compress, 56

computer, 48, 49, 72, 74, 112, 135, 149

contact, 17, 29, 40, 54, 60, 71, 83, 116, 122, 125

content, 3, 8, 11, 14, 38, 96, 115, 119, 120, 154

contests, 60, 117, 126

contract, 7, 9, 12, 37, 79

contributors, 129

control, 7, 8, 13, 58, 109

conversion, 52, 57, 104

convert, 52, 53, 57, 59, 137

copies, 47, 58, 89, 91, 92, 106, 126, 127, 128, 131, 145, 146, 151

copyright, 14, 71, 109, 110, 111, 112, 128, 146

country, i, 66, 108, 110, 112, 140

cover, 9, 11, 13, 16, 18, 49, 55, 59, 68, 69, 70, 71, 72, 75, 76, 77, 78, 92, 96, 99, 110, 116, 117, 121, 127, 130

CreateSpace, 59, 60, 63, 64, 84, 89, 91, 92, 93, 106, 132, 136

delivery, 53, 104, 108

deposit, 42, 133, 146, 147, 148

description, 32, 34, 59, 66, 93, 94, 95, 96, 100, 116, 122, 123, 129

design, 9, 11, 14, 16, 59, 61, 68, 69, 75, 76, 77, 127, 139, 141

developmental, 37, 38, 40, 139

devices, 51, 55, 85, 113, 152

dictionary, 152

digital formats, 53

Digital Rights Management, 112

disadvantages, 9

discount, 80, 104, 105, 106, 117

distribution, 11, 15, 16, 78, 85, 86, 88, 91, 92, 93, 103, 107, 108, 110, 144, 147

distributor, 59, 61, 63, 70, 85, 107, 109, 132

distributors, 15, 52, 59, 83, 84, 92, 108, 109, 128, 133

domain, 25, 73, 74, 112, 114, 117, 118, 119, 121, 140

Draft2Digital, 86, 132

DRM, 112, 113

earnings, 104, 133, 134

eBooks, 51, 53, 54, 55, 57, 85, 88, 92, 103, 113, 125, 126, 128, 140

edit, 18, 37, 39, 45

editing, 11, 16, 30, 34, 37, 38, 39, 41, 42, 44, 45, 48, 51, 59

editors, 30, 36, 37, 38, 40, 42, 48, 149

ellipses, 45, 57

email, 32, 83, 116, 118, 119, 121, 127, 133, 136, 145

encyclopedia, 152

equipment, 11, 13, 17, 135

errors, 38, 43, 47, 48, 90, 154

examples, 43, 148

experiences, 3, 4, 20, 21

Facebook, 116, 128, 131, 154

fee, 30, 42, 59, 72, 81, 89, 104, 108

feedback, 18, 27, 31, 37, 38, 41, 158

fiction, 23, 26, 98

file size, 53, 56, 104

files, 48, 53, 78, 90, 117, 130, 148, 149, 152, 154

financial, 8, 16, 17

font, 54, 55, 58, 59, 61, 63, 64, 74, 75

footer, 55

format, 31, 52, 55, 58, 61, 63, 81, 85, 110, 113, 130, 145, 146, 147

formats, 52, 53, 57, 64, 125, 129, 130, 144, 145, 146, 155

formatting, 11, 16, 51, 52, 54, 55, 56, 58, 61, 64, 65

forum, 29

forums, 31

freelancers, 9

giveaway, 60, 89, 126

goal, 17, 22, 26, 156, 157

Goodreads, 35, 125, 126, 130, 131

Google Play, 83, 87, 104, 105, 132

grammar, 30, 38, 44, 47, 151

group, 26, 35, 126

Guide, 52, 58

header, 55

headings, 55, 56, 62

homonyms, 49

hosting, 60, 114, 117, 118, 119, 120, 140

HTML, 53, 57, 96, 137

hyphenation, 55

hyphens, 64

iBooks, 84, 85, 87, 93, 133

idea, 20, 24, 111, 119, 154

images, 53, 56, 57, 62, 69, 71, 72, 73, 75

improve, 3, 29, 31, 71, 100

independent, 7

indie author, 7

information, i, 2, 3, 6, 23, 29, 43, 54, 66, 67, 78, 116, 121, 122, 123, 127, 128, 129, 134, 144, 145, 148, 154

IngramSpark, 63, 84, 86, 88, 91, 92, 93, 107, 133, 140

inspirations, 24, 27

instructions, 2, 70, 90, 119, 142, 145

intellectual property, 12, 71

interact, 126

interior, 61

Internet, 2, 6, 25, 36, 40, 51, 62, 71, 114, 117, 135, 151

invest, 10, 16, 114

investment, 8, 16, 41, 114, 142

ISBN, ii, 59, 66, 70, 93, 108, 109, 110, 123, 130, 140, 144

issues, 14, 16, 30, 34, 38, 52,

143

KDP, 54, 79, 81, 82, 83, 91, 92, 101, 104, 105, 123

KDP Select, 79, 82, 105

keywords, 99, 100, 101, 102, 129, 151

Kindle Countdown Deals, 80

Kindle Direct Publishing, 79, 84

Kindle Owners' Lending Library, 79

Kindle Unlimited, 79

knowledge, 1, 4, 6, 21, 22, 57, 115, 156, 160

Kobo, 84, 87, 113, 133

learn, 9, 10, 15, 16, 19, 23, 27, 38, 41, 57, 122, 142, 154, 156, 157

legal, i, 11, 16, 131, 146, 147, 148

librarians, 40

libraries, 1, 15, 61, 88, 91, 107, 108, 109, 144, 153

License, 66

licensing agreement, 71

licensing terms, 72, 75

lines, 37, 49, 64

links, i, 55, 85, 116, 122, 131

mailing list, 67, 116, 117, 118

management, 115, 152

manuscript, 7, 18, 22, 29, 31, 36, 37, 40, 42, 44, 45, 48, 51, 52, 57, 59, 63, 129

margins, 58, 63, 64

marketing, 4, 9, 10, 11, 13, 14, 15, 16, 55, 59, 60, 68, 99, 102, 105, 108, 115, 116, 117, 157

media kits, 116

mistakes, 39, 47, 48, 49

money, 2, 8, 11, 12, 14, 16, 17, 30, 79, 89, 114, 159, 160

non-breaking, 57

nonfiction, 23, 26, 98, 100

Nook, 83, 87, 133

novel, 19, 23, 29, 32, 111

novels, 102

objectives, 43

opinions, 24, 30, 41

page dimensions, 63

page numbers, 51, 58, 66, 67

page size, 64

paper, 49, 53, 61, 70

paragraph, 26, 33, 56, 57, 63, 64

parentheses, 49

PayPal, 121, 128, 133

PDF, 53, 55, 59, 64, 125, 129, 137

permafree, 105

plagiarism, 151, 152

platforms, 5, 7, 57, 79, 96, 110, 120, 151

practices, 3, 4

price, 8, 9, 14, 61, 70, 80, 91, 102, 103, 104, 105, 106, 107, 108, 132

pricing, i, 9, 13, 53, 61, 102,

103, 104, 106

principles, 3

print book, 19, 53, 54, 58, 59, 60, 61, 63, 64, 65, 66, 67, 69, 70, 72, 78, 85, 88, 91, 93, 96, 102, 106, 107, 110, 116, 126, 127, 129, 130, 140, 146

printer, 61, 70

printing services, 89, 90, 91

Print-on-demand, 58

process, 2, 3, 4, 5, 6, 8, 9, 13, 16, 22, 39, 41, 42, 44, 48, 59, 69, 78, 114

product pages, 60

profile, 116, 125, 129

profit, 8, 14, 53, 81, 91, 105, 106, 107, 132, 133

profit on sales, 8, 81

programming, 115

promote, 1, 15, 22

promotional, 72, 80, 91

promotions, 80, 103, 126

Pronoun, 86, 105

proof, 90, 130

proofread, 60

Proofread, 18, 48

Publish, i, 4, 18, 166

publisher, 7, 9, 10, 11, 12, 13, 16, 108, 109, 128, 129

publishing, 1, 2, 3, 4, 5, 6, 7, 8, 9, 10, 11, 12, 13, 15, 16, 17, 20, 22, 27, 60, 64, 99, 100, 108, 109, 112, 114, 115, 116, 130, 132, 149, 157, 159, 160

punctuation, 34, 38, 43, 47, 145

questions, 25, 31, 33, 38, 143

quotations, i, 56

rate, 42, 82, 103, 149

readers, 23, 29, 30, 51, 54, 60, 61, 62, 67, 71, 80, 81, 91, 99, 103, 105, 109, 113, 115, 117, 119, 123, 125, 126, 150, 157, 158, 166

readership, 10, 105, 115, 166

reading, 1, 20, 29, 33, 41, 42, 43, 48, 49, 51, 53, 55

recommendations, 40

reference, 3, 152, 153

references, 44

register, 111, 117, 118, 125, 128

report, 37, 40

research, 6, 23, 25, 41, 102

resolution, 62, 76, 98, 130

resources, 3, 18, 70, 160

retailers, 18, 53, 55, 66, 78, 79, 83, 85, 88, 89, 91, 92, 96, 102, 104, 105, 107, 108, 112, 116, 128, 129

retailer-specific, 55, 57, 85

review, i, 31, 67, 78, 123, 127, 130, 157

reviews, 24, 60, 93, 96, 126, 127, 129

risk, 11, 17

royalties, 8, 12, 14

royalty, 81, 103

sales, 14, 15, 23, 61, 71, 85, 91,
    93, 99, 104, 107, 133, 134,
    153, 154, 166
sample, 36, 45, 67, 92, 130
samples, 18, 125
save, 2, 30, 42, 56, 85
Schedule, 41
search, 25, 35, 40, 49, 50, 69,
    99, 100, 109, 110, 121, 123,
    152
self-publishing, 1, 2, 4, 7, 8, 12,
    13, 100
sell, 15, 60, 68, 78, 88, 100,
    104, 106, 107, 115, 116, 117
sentence, 26, 38, 48, 49
sentences, 20, 43, 48
serif, 55
services, i, 31, 59, 77, 85, 86,
    89, 90, 111, 118, 120, 145,
    148, 149
skills, 10, 11, 13, 42, 69, 142,
    160
Smashwords, 52, 58, 86, 88,
    91, 133
social media, 26, 31, 116, 122,
    128, 131, 151
software, 45, 52, 57, 74, 135,
    136, 151, 152
solution, 21
specification, 63
spelling, 30, 34, 38, 43, 47
spine, 59, 69
storage, 58, 148, 149
stores, 15, 17, 88, 91, 101, 105

stories, 22, 26, 43, 94
story, 19, 20, 23, 25, 29, 31, 33,
    38, 47, 94
storyline, 34
style, 25, 34, 37, 45, 47, 58, 93,
    160
subheadings, 56, 65
subjects, 25, 50
success, 12, 17, 83
suggestions, 29, 30, 31, 36,
    151, 157
summaries, 66, 147
tables, 53
tabs, 56, 57
tax, 127, 129, 134
template, 63, 70
text size, 61
thesaurus, 152
thumbnail, 69, 76
timing, 9, 13
tips, 18, 26, 142
title, 9, 13, 62, 82, 100, 105,
    108, 123, 128, 130, 145, 146,
    147
titles, 24, 65, 82, 88, 93, 128,
    150
tool, 60, 104, 129, 153, 154,
    155
tools, 2, 3, 7, 11, 13, 17, 80,
    102, 135, 151, 156, 160
topics, 24, 26, 150, 151, 152
tracks, 153
traditional, 7, 8, 9, 10, 12, 15
trends, 25, 153

trim size, 61

typefaces, 74, 75

verbs, 50

versions, 42, 55, 60, 69, 76, 95, 116

website, 32, 44, 52, 53, 62, 67, 69, 72, 81, 114, 115, 116, 117, 118, 119, 120, 121, 122, 123, 128, 131, 141, 152, 154, 156

websites, i, 3, 40, 53, 62, 71, 72, 75, 77, 115, 119, 130, 132, 160

wholesale pricing, 106

WordPress, 115, 118, 121

words, 9, 13, 20, 22, 24, 32, 41, 43, 47, 48, 62, 64, 93, 96, 100, 154, 155

working, 11, 17, 19, 38, 45, 142, 159

write, 7, 10, 12, 16, 18, 19, 20, 23, 24, 25, 26, 27, 41, 46, 52, 54, 100, 119, 159

writing, 1, 3, 9, 11, 16, 19, 21, 22, 24, 26, 27, 28, 30, 31, 34, 36, 38, 45, 52, 57, 61, 71, 98, 151, 160

Everything I Learned About

How to Market a Book

Make your self-publishing business more successful. Stop doing random acts of marketing and start following a solid plan to grow your business.

Whether you're just starting out or are an experienced author, this book is the easiest and fastest way to create a marketing plan that will boost your business growth.

You will discover in this radical book:

- Why "getting your name out there" is often a losing strategy
- Why short-term tactics don't produce consistent sales
- How to develop your own actionable marketing plan
- How to position your books for maximum discoverability
- How to apply marketing tactics effectively
- How to create a system that brings in a constant stream of ideal readers
- How to increase your readership by getting your book into libraries
- How to craft compelling messages and ads.

www.because.zone/because-self-publishing-works

NOTES